Life Of A Country Girl

By

Wanda Lehenbauer

M. LiClar Publishing Co., LLC
Monroe City, MO

ISBN: 0997024771
ISBN-13: 978-0-9970247-7-7

DEDICATION

This book is dedicated to my family, especially to my grandchildren as they maybe do not realize how things were year's ago. Over time, so many things have changed and sometimes it is hard to realize how it used to be

ACKNOWLEDGMENTS

I want to say thanks to Neal Minor for the help
you have given me in getting this published.

IN THE BEGINNING

Time, what you have so much of and yet not enough as you need more. How long have I thought of writing about my life as a farm gal growing up, and what it was like to live and yet so different from today. Thinking back, I remember starting to ask questions and having my mother to say, "You can ask more questions!" and yet how are you going to know if you don't ask them?

My parents, Willie Watts and Geraldine Elliott, were married April 11, 1924; secretly. They told of going together several years and when they decided to marry they thought they would just keep it secret for a while. They rode the train to Canton, MO and were married by a minister, Rev. H. E. Corbin, pastor of the M. E. Church South. (Methodist) No particular reason was given for not telling. The answer when I would ask was always the same, "We just wanted to." Mother was the only daughter of Jim and Rebecca (Douglas) Elliott who lived in the Gentry neighborhood and the farm where Bennie and Julia (Mette) Lehenbauer lived for years and now owned by Mitch and GiGi Lehenbauer. Bennie and Julia purchased it from my mother, and their children Doris and Chris were very small at the time. Dad lived on the Watts' farm where 10 of the 12 children were born. The first two were born on the hill north of the Watts Homestead. His parents were John Martin and Mary Catherine (Baxter) Watts. Dad purchased the Watts place from the others and lived there for a few years with his mother until after her death in 1922. This house was built by his dad in 1881, located in Ralls County, MO between Center, MO and Monroe City, MO. A rather large house with eight rooms in all and very well built. It wasn't more than needed as there was such a large family. His dad started working at the age of ten and was a very successful farmer. To this union the following children were born; Iona, Lera, David, Baxter, Lonley, Una, Ella, Willie, Angelia, Etra, and Lillian. One died in infancy. It was told that she didn't have a doctor with any of the children. Another thing I was told about Grandmother Watts was that they never saw her mad about anything. That is quite a compliment -- with eleven? She had to be a "Saint" to say the least if you never get angry and have eleven living children.

My dad was a very hard worker and he farmed with horses to put out a crop. Mother worked at home, sewing and putting out a garden among other things. They attended Ariel church and took part in things in the community. After four years trying to get ahead, I was born August 20, 1928. I remember mother telling of Dr. Pipkin coming from Monroe City on the train and was with her until I appeared. He rode the train, so he had to come to Huntington and then probably by horse and buggy the rest of the way. That would be at least five miles. My aunt, Alma Watts (Baxter's wife) was there to help in the delivery. I weighed a scant seven pounds and was named Wanda Marie with the initials of my dad, W. M. The Wanda was after a girl that was Ruth Holt's daughter, a friend who lived in New London, MO. Everything was pretty vague as to the happenings after I was born.

Dad was a person that it was hard to get him to talk. I was always asking him questions and he would just shrug his shoulders. Many times, he just wouldn't answer, and I would go to mother with the question only to find out not much more, as she wouldn't explain things either. Shall I say I was always curious as to why and what happened. Sometimes I got answers and sometimes I didn't. So many things now that should have been explained and weren't, and I was in the world of trying to learn and without words or books you had no way to learn. Books were one thing we didn't have, not even a good dictionary to look up a word. I could not find enough to do, you could only spend so much time with dolls and then on to something else. There were no puzzles, pictures to color, and it was mostly make believe. I know that I was two when I got a little sister, which caused more questions. No answers that satisfied me. Ha! I must have been the mean little girl that didn't seem to ever get my curiosity taken care of.

I know I enjoyed my grandparents, my mother's parents, as they were the only grandparents that I had, for Dad's parents had died before they ever married. I remember going to their place, but I was very small. I remember the candy grandpa would buy which was coconut bonbons, and a ribbon candy soft with chocolate, vanilla and strawberry put to form a rectangle. They also bought peanuts. I am sure they enjoyed their only grandchildren. No wonder our time together was so very special.

Thinking back, I was almost two when my little sister arrived June 25, 1930. She was named Rebecca Jean. Rebecca was after mother's mother who was Rebecca Ann. I am sure Dr. Pipkin was the doctor and of course you didn't know anything until the little girl arrived. Such things weren't talked about and so I just took it all in and said nothing. The weather was warm then and I am sure I was entertained with other things. We usually had a dog and a cat or two but not too many as dad didn't want to feed them. I maybe was with my grandparents, who knows.

I remembered getting all dressed up in our new dresses after a year or so to go somewhere. Most of them mother had made. How she spent hours at the sewing machine working on them. No pictures were taken of us until I was 5 and Jean 3. I asked why, and she said it was too expensive to have a camera. People did without in order to save money to have for the essentials you would need in everyday life. I would always remind her that Aunt Alma had a camera, if she can have one we can too, so I thought. Aunt Alma was Baxter Watts' wife and she lived a half mile south of our place.

At home I remember we had wood stoves to heat the house and no indoor plumbing. You would hope that there was a pot in the house for the night time use; for in the daytime you had to go outside to the toilet, a two or three-holer and a catalog for paper. How we would crunch the paper in a small wad in order to make it softer. What a chill when it was cold, and you would make a run. We had to go through the chicken yard gate and north to that powerful little building.

Dad always milked a cow or two, so we would have plenty of milk and we sold cream after it was put in the separator, and that, with the eggs we gathered usually brought us enough money that we were able to buy our groceries. For those that don't know what a separator is, it was a small tank that was on legs and had a top that covered the container. The cream would rise to the top and every day you had to drain all of the milk away at the bottom and then the cream was put in a can for selling. In the summer you had to keep the cream sweet in order to sell it. Cream was taken to a place in Monroe City called Henderson's to sell and your eggs were taken there also. Milk was also put into a crock every day or most every day for our use. Cream would be skimmed off the top and this was saved and when you had enough you churned it for butter. We had a large jar that you put the cream in and the churn that went on top of the jar. This had a paddle on one end and a top and crank on the other and you turned the crank until butter appeared. Sometimes it took a long time and sometimes it didn't. After the butter showed in the milk from churning it was removed and washed to get all of the milk out of the butter. It was then put in a dish and put on ice for later use when needed. If the cows were dry and not giving milk than you had to buy oleo for use and it was always white and had to have color put in the oleo for it to be yellow. So, with the oleo you always got a little bit of color on a piece of cardboard to work in the oleo or margarine.

We had some cows, horses, hogs, sheep and chickens. How I would love it when a new lamb was born and brought into the house to get in from the cold, and dad would fix the lamb up with some warm milk and a little whiskey to give it some extra strength. He would call the drink a toddy. Oh, how soft and cuddly the little lamb would be, and I would get to pet them, especially if dad would bring one inside, that needed a little milk and warmth. But when it began to move around, out it would go back to its mommy to be fed more and to make its' way into the world. Once in a while a calf was brought in for the same reasons, a cold night and needing a little warmth and fed a little to get a start in life. Dad would put a little whiskey in the milk for both lambs and calves to help them on their way to living if they seemed weak and needed a little help to get started.

Then in the spring the sheep would always have to be sheared. The weather would get too warm for them to have all of that wool on and usually dad had someone to help him and they would spend a day or so shearing sheep. I always liked going down to the barn and seeing how they would do it. Many times, mother had other ideas as to what I should be doing, and lots of time she didn't want me to go. I didn't understand that. The wool would be sold at certain places in Monroe City and sometimes he would get quite a bit for the amount he had. Wool was sent to places where the wool was made into fabric and then clothing.

Laundry was very different also. All of the water had to be carried inside and for some time she used tubs and a scrub board to get things clean. Later, she did have a washer with a motor on it run by a gasoline motor. This motor mother started by using her foot pressing down on a pedal that started the machine. That was better than scrubbing by hand. Lye soap was used and was made by mother using lard from the hogs that were butchered and lye, someway done with a recipe that formed and was cut in squares to be used to clean the clothes. They didn't have the soaps like Tide and many others to clean clothes with. Also, some things needed to be starched and so Argo starch was made by putting the powder in water and heating it until it thickened. That way dad's shirts were starched as well as many other things. Bluing was also added to the last rinse tub another whitening agent. So, wash day was not a quick thing as it took all day for all of this to get done. Clothes were hung outside on the line and if in cold weather they were hung there also or inside. When weather didn't permit her to hang outside they would put up lines in the house, especially behind the stove to put the clothes on to dry. Mother's ironing was done with flat irons heated on the stove and later she had a gas iron and special gas added, as well as air had to be pumped in the tank, for her to be able to iron. Also, clothes had to be sprinkled and rolled up and covered with a towel in order for them to be ironed. The clothes were mainly cotton and if you didn't dampen the material you would have a very wrinkled garment.

In the winter the only heat we had was the cook stove in the kitchen and another stove in the dining room and that heated the bedroom downstairs. Jean and I had to make our way upstairs in the cold and sleep on an old feather bed to keep warm. Once in a while mother would heat cloths and put them in bed with us to put our feet on. I hated the feather bed as you made a hole or indentation in the mattress and sometimes you couldn't get out as you were in there mighty deep. To get upstairs we had to take a flashlight or a candle as our only source of light. You had to hope you didn't need to go to the toilet or that you didn't feel well in the night. If this did happen you had to go downstairs or call mother for help. She always had a chamber to use, which was usually white enamel or granite.

If we ever had company at our house and needed to use the living room, then we had to build another fire in the stove. Lamps had to be carried in there also. You see, to get to the living room back then, you had to go through the bedroom or the front hall where the stairway was. So, you didn't ask for things like that, your parents wouldn't like it and you just dealt with the darkness and cold if in the winter, unless you had company.

For lights we used kerosene lamps and they sure weren't the best to see by. There was no television, only radio and games, dolls and sometimes we would play paper dolls cut from the catalogue, as mother wouldn't buy us any. Sure had a hard time getting the clothes cut out in the catalogue to match a lady that was found in the catalogue with another outfit on. There weren't many games either, but a few. Sometimes we would play 'Old Maid' with the playing cards and the joker would be the 'Old Maid.' How my sister would hate to be the 'Old Maid.' That was not fun for her, she wanted me to be the 'Old Maid, which was okay. She always wanted to do what she wanted to do, when she wanted to do it.

FIRST THOUGHTS OF SCHOOL

When I was about five in 1933 our thoughts were "when do we go to school?" Linwood school was about two miles from my home. Due to the teacher having so many grades you had to either start an even year, or an uneven year. It was up to the parents. I was five in August and mother knew if she started me that year I would go straight through otherwise I would have to skip grades. Lloyd started an uneven year and he had to take the first four grades than skip to the sixth, then fifth, eighth and seventh. Mother did not want me to wait until I was seven, so she started me when I was five, so I wouldn't skip. She thought that was very hard on kids. So, I was to go in September after being five on August 20th. School was only for eight months from September to April. That was a long way for me to walk to school, but mother was determined, and I started, would walk by myself to Lloyd's, my first cousin, which was at least a half mile and then we would walk together the rest of the way. We were able to go through a wooded area, which cut off at least a half mile and that helped a lot. I was so glad to have Lloyd to walk with and Virginia Baynum was my first-grade school teacher. I guess one of the reasons Lloyd and I were so close is because we had to be buddies to meet our many challenges in life on the road to school. We had to go by a lady's house that lived by herself, she had a bull that had horns that pawed the dirt clear over his head and a dog that was jumping high and barking that would frighten you no matter how big you were! This poor lady walked with a limp and always had men's pants on and an old felt hat. Sometimes we would get so scared that we thought the bull, or the dog would get us for sure. A short distance from the bull and dog was where you enter the wooded area we liked to walk through and come out across from the school. Bud McClintock's lived across the road and sometimes we would go over that way to get away from all the commotion; it at least made us feel better.

Our school was a one -room building with a hall across the front of the building where children hung their coats and hats. Our heat was from a large stove with a heavy jacket around the outside. The teacher had to put wood in the stove for us to have heat. If it got too hot, we had to open a window. All of us had desks to sit at and of course the teacher had her large desk also. When the weather was bad outside we had to play games inside for our recess period.

None of the rural schools had running water, you had to bring your own drinking liquid, and no bathrooms. There were toilets outside, one for the boys and one for the girls and quite a distance for each of us to run to get there. We had a ball field outside in the back where we would play baseball and sometimes we would play dodge ball. I remember one day either my first or second grade, someone put pepper on top of the stove and we all began sneezing and coughing and finally the teacher had to stop class and figure out "who did that"? It turned out to be a big boy in one of the upper grades and my, but he did get a slapping. I was so glad it wasn't me! I really felt sorry for the teacher as she was in charge of so many grades, she had to see that everyone learned, and did it in a short time. She had to keep the fire burning and sweep the floor after a day at school whether she did it the evening or the morning before school started. She had to keep track of everyone's grades and try to keep order and everyone happy. When I started there were several guys that were really tall, strong boys.

I had a little problem at least mother thought so, I was told I had to use my right hand for writing as nothing was made for a left-handed person. I'd try and when no one was looking I would put the pencil back in the left hand and try to write. That right one didn't work very well, and I told her so, but she was after me constantly to change. I finally made it writing with my right hand but it wasn't easy, that is for sure. To this day I'm a mixed-up affair, I write right handed but throw a ball with my left hand, I bat right handed and the list goes on and on. Years and years later I remember Lloyd saying "Wanda, why do you always go to the left when going up or down stairs or anywhere?" My reply was "I don't know, I didn't know I did." Now I realize that it is because I am so left handed that it seems natural for me to do that but I'm sure some people think it strange.

I remember going to Monroe City on our weekly trip for groceries and to take our eggs, maybe cream. There was talk that some kids in Monroe had measles, roseola, scarlet fever or the mumps. Mother would tell Jean and I we had to stay in the car, so we would not catch anything. That was a pain to say the least. Go to town and have to stay in the car? That wasn't any fun! But if she said we had to that was the order we had to keep. We would try to get her to promise us something if we had to do that. Sometimes she did and sometimes she didn't. You never knew how it was going to turn out.

There was one time in the dead of winter, when trees were breaking because of ice and to my surprise mother said, "I could go to school." I left quickly and when I got over to Uncle Baxter's hill I could not hold my feet because it was so very slick. I had been holding on to the branches on the side of the road, but when I got near the top there were no branches to hold on to. After several tries, Lloyd was getting impatient. We were needing to leave, so I just got down and crawled up the next 5-6 feet of distance, as there was no other way. When we got to Wike's woods we knew that to go around the road was up and down hills and we would not make it that way, so we went through Wike's woods as we normally did. We could hear the branches of the trees breaking and popping as we traveled along, and we would take turns holding up the branches for the other one to go through and that was quite an experience, but we made it. We were so proud of ourselves.

Linwood school was on a hill, and when the snow was on we would get to go sled riding down the hill at the school. That was always such fun and a joy. I felt so lucky, Lloyd was my dear friend. He let me use his sled too. I always wanted a sled but only had the one that dad made which was nice but so heavy it was hard to get it to take you anywhere. In fact, it was impossible to take it anywhere. So, it was not much use as dad made it out of an old school slide. If it hadn't been for Lloyd I wouldn't have been able to do much of anything as when it came to sleds and bikes. I would never have learned how as I couldn't have one no matter when I asked.

LOSS OF LOVED ONES

In January the year 1934, my grandfather Elliott got very sick and mother was there to help take care of him for several weeks. I remember mother staying up there nights and I would ride back and forth with dad going down to milk the cow and taking care of the stock. Sometimes Jean and I would go to Aunt Angelia Bixler's. Aunt Angelia was dad's sister and they lived near my grandparents. We spent some time there as mother needed help in taking care of us. Dad was able to make it by himself. This seemed forever to me as a little girl and things were not getting better. Then Grandfather Elliott died on January 17th and after that grandmother went to bed sick and she died seventeen hours later. That was quite a shock for me to believe it could happen. Why did they die so soon and why did both of them die? That was really hard to understand. I couldn't believe it! How could this happen? The only grandparents I had, and both were gone! Remember I was only five years old when this happened and hard for a five-year-old to understand what happened!

Grandfather had a flu-like sickness and grandmother was sick a short time and she didn't last long, probably nearly the same thing. I don't think that any doctor said exactly what they had but they didn't have medicines back than that they do now and that is just the way it was back in the thirties. Mother being the only child had to make all of the arrangements. Back then they didn't take the bodies to a funeral home but instead laid them in caskets and kept them in the house. Mother kept getting rid of Jean and I and we were sent to Aunt Angelia's to spend some time there, so she could get things done. I really couldn't understand that because I knew I would be good, just didn't know about Jean, she was a busy body for sure.

The bodies were placed in the living room in their caskets and the funeral was held a day or so later. This was in January and a nice day for January. The day of the funeral the house was full of people and so was the yard. The service was held in the house. So many friends came to give their respects to the family. Mother thought I was too small to understand but I remembered it all even to the dress that mother wore. The dress was black with sheer material for the sleeves with a velvet design over the sheer material. It was a beautiful dress! I remember chairs being set up in the dining room area and probably other areas also. During the service there was a loud "Pop" and the big china cabinet started to topple over and several grabbed it and kept it from falling on the floor. The china was full of dishes and many of them were hand painted china. We discovered after the funeral and burial that the loud pop was a floor joist breaking due to so much weight in the house. Guess it was lucky that more things didn't happen, but they didn't. This was something I will never forget as it was unbelievable to have watched all of this.

The best I can remember is that we always had a car and even though the roads were not great they were mostly graveled, and we would bump all the way to Monroe City, Center, New London and Hannibal or where ever you might be going.

After my Grandparents service and burial that meant that all of the things in the house had to be removed to the Watts place where we lived. One of the first pieces was that large upright piano made by Smith's and Barnes, was brought to where we lived and placed in the living room. This room I previously talked about where there wasn't any heat and no lights. I thought about this big thing and wondered if I could ever learn to play. Do you suppose it is possible? I decided to try when I could and hopefully I would be able to do that. I started practicing and trying to pick out pieces. Mother would hum or sing pieces or maybe I would hear them on the radio, and so I started going into the room sometimes in the daylight and sometimes in the dark. Sometimes when I was so bored I would go in and find the bench and scoot on that to what I thought was the center and then try to find middle C, which was in the center. Then to try to find the right note for the pitch I was trying on the piece I was thinking of. One that mother was singing, or I would hear it on the radio. I was so surprised as to what I could do. It was astonishing in fact. Do you suppose I could do that? I kept practicing and getting very determined and told mother that I was going to learn to play like a lady by the name of Lucille Moyer, who lived in the neighborhood and was pianist at the Ariel Christian Church. She was really very good and how I dreamed I would be like her and someday play. As years passed I knew Mother would not buy the sheet music and so I would get the booklets that had only the words of the pieces in them and if you knew the melody than you could apply the words. What a challenge!! My sister would laugh at me and while her words bothered me, I kept on paying no attention. Years later mother did consent to give me piano lessons and I worked so hard on trying to play by note but I didn't like that as well, as it didn't sound like I wanted it to sound. Little by little it got better, and I have never given up my love for music and practice almost every day.

GOING TO CHURCH – AND THE WAY IT WAS

We attended Ariel church. They had Sunday school every Sunday but only services once a month. Mother and Dad wouldn't take me every Sunday but if I could get over to Aunt Alma's and Uncle Baxter's I could go—for they seldom missed. The Watts family had taken part in the Ariel Christian Church for many years and that was the nearest church and one in the neighborhood. Aunt Alma and Uncle Baxter liked to go to Sunday school and mother and dad didn't. This church was just west of the Linwood School and still standing and they still have services there.   Rev. John Golden was the minister for years. I remember when Lloyd was probably ten or eleven he and several others joined church and after school one day, Rev.Golden and the ones that had come forward in the service all gathered I think at a place at Salt River. Rev Golden baptized the people in the river. That was so very impressive to me and how I wished I was one of them and felt very drawn to join them but wasn't for sure how mother would react so refrained to do so. When I told mother she said why? And my answer was you say no so many times, I felt that might be the answer this time. I finally joined church while in my high school days, and at another church. The minister begged me so much I finally gave in, but my heart was not in it like it should have been. Later the family went back to Ariel. This was all because of some tension in the community and later we were back at Ariel and taking part in the community things.

Many times, after mother teaching me chords, Jean and I would sing hymns and other music. Many times, we were asked to sing at church services at Ariel and at Huntington Christian Church. This was fun, but yet a little scary as we weren't very big. Most of the time it went okay but only encouragement came from mother, not dad, he never bragged or said anything good or bad. You never knew what he thought. Some ministers would brag on us, which made us feel good, sometimes I wondered if they really meant it, but they asked over and over.

Dad liked to campaign for candidates and so we would go to ice cream suppers to eat and for dad to talk and mother to visit. The nights got mighty long waiting and sometimes my legs would just give out, I can remember dad holding me a few nights, and that was always great. I remember going to the Brush Creek chicken dinner and that was nice too. There were so many children there and I remember begging to go, as it would be fun. I remember a family coming there, in a big truck just full of boys and girls and most of them were bare-foot. Not everyone had shoes those days. I was always glad I did for dress up but didn't for every day I had to go barefoot too until I was a good-sized girl in early teens I was always stepping on a rock, a thistle or something, and that hurt so bad. If I ever got my shoes wet when they dried they were stiff as boards. The answer was always NO! for a new pair of shoes.

Growing up with my sister was sometimes a great challenge, as knowing she was the youngest she would take advantage of that and act like she was hurt when she wasn't. She was constantly wanting her way, and if it was something she knew she did and didn't want a spanking, she wouldn't tell the truth, and mother would believe her. She would go bragging about it and I would have to take the consequences. That was sure hard to take many times. She loved to climb, and I didn't, and so again she would keep after me until I did climb, and then I couldn't get down without spraining my ankle, so it was one thing after another and she wasn't supposed to be up there in the first place.

Dad would go to Palmyra to a cattle and hog sale on Mondays, ever so often, and would be gone all day. He would leave early and come home late and that was always so strange to me, but it happened over and over. Mother would be so worried she would walk the floor. All other days he would be working on the farm from sun up to sun down.

When school was canceled that meant everyone had to get the word by phone as there was no other way to let people know. Radio gave you the weather forecast but nothing else as to the school closing. Everyone had to do it on their own, or your neighbor had to get you the word.

For lights we had kerosene lamps and they sure weren't the best to see by. There was no television, only radio run by battery, and games, dolls and sometimes we would play paper dolls cut from the catalog as mother wouldn't buy us any. Sure had a hard time getting the clothes cut out in the catalog to match a lady that was found in the catalog with another outfit. This was almost impossible.

Mother finally bought an Aladdin lamp. The one I now use in my bedroom near my bed. This I made into an electric lamp, but I still have the mantle and special shade that the lamp required to burn kerosene. This lamp was very good to see to read, or most anything you wanted to do that required a good light. We only had one of these and the rest were the regular kerosene lamps. We probably didn't have more than four lamps in all. There were certain programs that were on radio that I always enjoyed. One was "Fibber Magee and Molly." You would have to listen to the program for every night they were on, Fibber would always open the closet door, and you never heard the like of stuff falling from the closet as you would hear falling from theirs. It was so funny! Another program was "Name that Tune" and that was always fun to guess the tunes they were playing. Then there was a love story of a couple that had twins, a boy and a girl. Their names were Kit and Kathy. I always said that I was going to have a little girl someday and would name her Kathy and I did. But to use Kit for a child Ivan didn't think much of that name. I used to tease him that he had most of his dogs named girl's name that he liked.

MY BUDDY NEXT DOOR

As I grew older I wanted to go see Lloyd, who was the son of Baxter and Alma Watts. Baxter was dad's brother and so that made Lloyd and I first cousins. They lived just south of my home about a half a mile or so and he was a year older than me. He had some new things to play with and that was of interest. Lloyd had two older sisters, Mary Sue and Dorothy and they were always gone to school or somewhere, at least it seemed that way. They were both much older than he and found out later that he had an older brother that died from getting too close to the fireplace and caught his flannel gown on fire and inhaled the fumes so much that he died when only eighteen months old. That was a sad thing to learn. Also, in order for Mary Sue and Dorothy to get their high school education they had to stay in Monroe City in an apartment. That really sounded grown up to stay in an apartment, Gee! I wondered if I would have to do that -- life ahead was a mystery.

I remember making up an excuse to go see Lloyd when I had heard his sisters were having some girlfriends in, and I wanted to see what they looked like and what they were doing and wearing. I remembered those people for years to come, all in the eyes of a wee little girl.

Sometimes while visiting Lloyd he would be drawing cars or scenery. That was fun. I loved to draw, and he got pastels to draw with and paper, which I didn't seem to ever have except paper at school. Nothing for drawing. Lloyd one time had what they call charcoal and I loved it all, and we would sit by the hour and draw. I did more scenery than anything else, but a lot of my ideas were from watching Lloyd. Several times at home I would draw characters in the newspaper. One time I did draw Henry, and he didn't have any clothes on and I thought mother was going to whip me, and I said, "Mother it is in the paper!"

She said, "that doesn't matter. You had no business drawing pictures like that." Trouble. I seemed to be in trouble even when I tried not to.

I thought a tricycle would be nice to have and finally got one for Christmas. Jean and I had to share it and we did and another time we did get a wagon, which was given in order to carry in wood, it was large and heavy, and not much fun to say the least. We would argue as to whose turn it was to haul in the wood, Jean didn't like doing jobs. She would always say it was my turn when it was hers, and she didn't want to do it.

Summertime meant playing outside, going after the milk cows, as they had to be milked both morning and evening. It also meant going barefoot and I did detest that as I was always getting a sticker in my foot or having a crawdad in the cow path that pinched my foot. Some nights we would have to walk a long way to find the two milk cows, as there was always some hill they could hide behind and that made us have to walk a long way to get them in. I used to say, "Mother can't you buy me something to wear on my feet that has a sole?" In the winter it was use the wagon and carry in the wood for heat and that was hard work also. We heated with wood stoves and wood had to be carried in every night to have heat. We didn't get electricity until 1938, and no water in the house until 1941. Aunt Alma and Uncle Baxter had what they called the Delco system and with that they had electric lights. I was always asking, "How come they can have electricity and we can't"? I was always given an off answer and make the most of it as dad didn't want to spend the money for that. I remember they had water in the house also. Their home was so different from mine with lights and water. They even had a bathtub and stool. What a dream!

Baths were taken about twice a week in the wintertime. Summer was a little more often. A large tub that was used for washing clothes was put behind a stove and water heated and my sister was always first and I was second and had to use the same wash water. I must always give in because she was the youngest. That didn't always make me happy. Some things you just had to accept.

WHAT MEAT DID WE HAVE?

In the fall or early winter, we would butcher hogs and mother would can the meat. I remember the quarts of meat she did, mainly sausage and ribs and always so much fat in the jar with the meat. That grease always bothered me, and I really didn't like eating the sausage or the ribs because of that. To this day I really don't think much of ribs for meat but occasionally they are good, if they aren't greasy. They did rub a mixture on the hams and shoulders and they were hung in the smoke house to be used at a later date.

We always put out a few chickens and in the summer some of them would be dressed and we would have chicken for our meat. Many times, we would dress the chicken, and then fry it. My thoughts were, "let's wait another day to have the chicken, but that didn't work." In order to dress the chickens if more than one was done we would have to heat the water, and while it was heating we would have to catch the chicken and kill it. That was done most of the time by putting a stick on its head and pulling the head off. Sounds gruesome, but it worked and better than taking a hatchet and trying to kill them that way. Then you had to fix a container of hot water to dip the chicken in and then pull all of the feathers off and then the chicken was taken inside and put in more water to be cleaned and cut apart for frying. Seemed we were always running out of water, and more had to be carried in by the bucket from our cistern which was our only water supply.

Occasionally we had squirrel or rabbit but not too often. However, one summer we had lots of rabbits in the wheat and I got so tired of having rabbit, I didn't know what to do. We had rabbits in the refrigerator, and in about everything you could think of, as there were so many. Remember they didn't have freezers then and did I ever get tired of eating rabbit!

17

Mother also canned vegetables from our garden, especially green beans. In the spring we had peas and by fall we had potatoes to use. They were all very good to eat and a change rather than the same old thing over and over. Sometimes the menu just didn't change. Mother always fixed dad gravy for breakfast and many times she woke me up scraping the skillet, to get the gravy in the bowl for breakfast. I would say, "I hope if I ever get married, I don't have to fix gravy every morning for my husband!"

Some of my time was spent making mud pies, and in the world of make believe was sort of fun. What you didn't think of to make your project to look as good as possible! We played house many days and that would last for a while and then on to find something else. Going to the creek was a no, no, as we might fall in and drown. Lots of restrictions!

If we ever went to the carnival I would come home and try some of the stunts I would see them do such as rolling on a barrel. Falling from that wasn't any fun. Sometimes you would try to fix a paddle and find an old hoop and try guiding that hoop with the paddle. That wasn't too bad. Dad was never interested in putting up a swing and for some reason swings and I didn't fare very well either. I could only stay in the porch swing a short time and then my head wouldn't take any more of that.

Some of the games that we would play as kids in school or at home was Red Light, Hot Potato, Hide and Go Seek to mention a few. Sometimes we would lay on the ground and look at the shapes of the clouds and try to guess what they were in the shape of. Some things we had was Kool-Aide drinks, sometimes we would laugh about something until your stomach would hurt so bad. We never had people shooting themselves like they do now. Parents taking you to a cafeteria was a "Big Deal." That seldom happened! There weren't any computers, and you studied books to learn or the teacher or parents taught you. There were never very many books in our house as that was one thing mother didn't buy. A few times we went to the library in Monroe City. Mother loved to read, but it was different with Jean and I as far as reading material, we weren't supposed to read or something. I did use the library at school but not a big selection.

There were some black people in the community such as at Sidney, which is south of Huntington. I have a picture of an old rock house over my piano and I bought that picture as it reminded me so much of Sidney and the way it looked several years ago. I'm sure white people lived in there first, but later blacks lived there also. There was another house on the corner where John McElroy lived. He was raised across the road in the big two-story house, and for years the black people were the ones that worked for McElroy's, doing field work and many other jobs. I've been there when it was meal time and the blacks would be eating on the porch. No one thought anything about it and of course I was always wondering why? Why were they eating by themselves? When we would go to my Aunt Una Hager's for wheat threshing the blacks would be eating on the porch. The answers were all the same, they wanted to do that, and were always treated well by people.

Another thing I remember about the black people is that in the small town of New London, MO, just south of Hannibal, that when you would go to the court house in getting there you would see chair after chair with black people sitting there most of the day. Most of them were men and while there, they were always talking. I guess most of them didn't have jobs for they were always on the streets. That was always hard for me to understand. Then in Center, MO it was told that a black man was not allowed. However, I never knew them to have one there, which was always strange to me. Monroe City had plenty of black people, but you didn't see them on the streets. They were always busy doing something or in their homes. I never knew any of them to be abused, in any way, they were always respected. To this day there is a black cemetery at Brush Creek Catholic Church, where the slaves were buried.

Saturday was our day for going to Monroe City for groceries. I would manage to get a nickel or dime from mother for an ice cream cone and such a delight and be so careful not to get any on my dress, but Jean would usually manage to get it down her front. Once in a while we could get a sack of candy and my sister just couldn't leave it alone, she usually consumed three-fourths of the sack and then deny that she did. From baby on she was always trying to get by with something and she usually did. Seemed mother always believed her, no matter what I said. Another thing we did was to go to the gas station and fill up. Back then the attendant would come out of the station, fill your car, clean the windshield and check the oil. Now you do it yourself without help. Also, when you would get home after purchasing laundry soap or maybe oatmeal you might have a dish inside of the box. That was quite interesting, and many times certain things were bought in order to have more glassware.

One Saturday dad was working; so mother, my sister and I went to Monroe to get some groceries. We had a flat tire on the car and while mother was working on the tire, changing it, near the McElroy house where the negro's lived. My sister looked up and said, "Oh Mom! Here comes a big, fat nigger down the road!"

Mother said, "Hush, you shouldn't talk like that!"

Jean didn't say anymore and when he got near, it was Bill Allen, a very respected black man that mother knew well. Mother apologized for Jean's remark, and he said, "That's alright Miss Geraldine." And, he stood there until the tire was fixed and we were on our way. He was a very nice gentleman.

Medicine was something that you had only a few things that were used a lot. If your bowels weren't working just so, out would come the castor oil. My, did I hate that stuff. It was terrible! I never ran from my mother until she got out that bottle and it was the worst tasting stuff I ever tasted! She always had something to help get rid of the taste, but nothing worked in my thinking. My sister never had the problems I did, and I saw that bottle way too often. If you ever cut your hand mother would get out the iodine and Lysol and she would pour Lysol down on the sore and then paint it with iodine. One time I cut my hand on the lawnmower blade and it was fairly deep. And out came mother with both bottles. It stung a bit, but usually we didn't get it infected so that was good.

We never had beef to eat it was always pork or chicken. Every week the ice man, who was first Mr. Chisham, brought us ice. We had an old ice box that held 50 or 100-pound cakes of ice in the special cabinet for the cooling of our milk and other foods. I can remember the Chisham family, who traveled in an old truck with a loud exhaust popping as it traveled along and had kids of all sizes riding inside and out and, on the back, coming down the hill hollering and that was a sight to see as well as hear. Later on, they gave it up and a man by the name of Walter Roland was our ice man. He and his parents had the store at Spalding. He would bring us ice as well as a few groceries, like bread and milk. He was always a great man to see and was always happy and would give his big laugh that you could hear for a long distance. Bread was maybe ten cents a loaf and ice maybe fifty cents. Sometimes mother would bring the ice home with her from town wrapped up in a blanket depending on her need and her trips for groceries. We had milk cows but if they had just had calves we would have to wait until later on to have milk as the calves needed the milk.

THE EVERYDAY LIFE AND MORE HAPPY TIMES

Our roads were mostly graveled, and we would bump all the way to Monroe, Center, New London or wherever might be going. So many times, after going to Monroe or somewhere else where I would ride for miles in the back seat of the car would have such a headache when we got home. No one ever mentioned, that it might be car sickness nothing seemed to change, and that was something I had to put up with no matter what.

I remember trying to stay awake when we would go see Alfred and Elizabeth Neville, who lived a few miles away and the four of them would play cards. I'd try my best to stay awake as she would always have refreshments and I was always ready to try some goodies that she would fix. They were always so good to eat and was nice when they did something different, or to go someplace different was wonderful! There were many other couples that they played with besides the ones that went to the card parties.

Dad liked to campaign for candidates and so we would go to ice cream suppers to eat and for dad to talk and mother to visit. The nights got mighty long waiting and sometimes my legs would just give out, can remember dad holding me a few nights and that was always special. I remember going to the Brush Creek chicken dinner and that was nice also for there were so many children there and I remember begging to go as it would be fun. I remember a family coming there in a big truck just full of boys and girls and most of them were bare-foot. Not everyone had shoes those days. I was always glad I did but didn't for every day. I had to go barefoot too, until I was a good-sized girl in early teens.

When I was small and growing up I remember we had a phone. It was a wooden box and it hung on the wall and you had to ring the operator and they would ring the party you were calling. There were as many as eight on the party line. If someone did a lot of talking you couldn't use the phone. You could listen in on their conversation and that was done lots of times. Later on, you finally had four or five on your line. It was terrible if you had to make a long distance phone call. That was forbidden as it cost money to do that. The phone was a forbidden tool for children. You could only talk to people in the community, and not many people around with kids. Lloyd was about all I had. I remember trying to visit Reva McClintock and she said she had too much work to do to play, so I visited only once, and she never visited me. Linwood school was located south of my house, probably about two miles. One of our fun times was in the winter when the snow was on we would get to go sled riding down the hill there at the school. That was always such fun and a joy and I was lucky that Lloyd was my dear friend and he let me use his sled too. I always wanted a sled but only had the one that dad made which was nice but so heavy it was hard to get it to take you anywhere. So, it was not much use and was made out of an old school slide. We had some mighty big snows in the winter, sometimes several feet deep and that was a job to walk with it so deep. Sometimes the snow was way up on the fence posts, so you knew that it would be hard to walk. I always had boots to wear but sometimes the snow would get inside of the boot and then my feet would be very cold.

I remember that the Griffin girl had a pony to ride. She was a big girl and the pony was so loaded down with all of the gear that she had it was almost too much for her to ride the pony even in cold weather. We had a shed at school for the ponies. She was not the only one to ride, but the only one that rode while I was going. Most of us just walked. Once in a while mother or dad would come for us but very seldom. We walked in all kinds of weather and some of the things mother had me wear were very warm but very often I would be very sweaty with perspiration, think I was more likely to get a cold by being too warm. Slacks were only worn under your dresses not as the usual wear. Long stockings were also worn, and they were quite a pain to keep up as garters didn't work very well on skinny legs. Ha! I remember once or twice that Dad walked to school, and we walked together home. I always wondered why he didn't bring the car but for some reason he thought it was better to walk. I didn't always get a lot of answers when I would ask a question. Think I forgot the long underwear we had to wear also. That was quite a pain to get on and off when necessary. I remember that I would really think I was free when spring arrived and I could leave the underwear and long stockings at home. Hurray! I was free to run, and it felt so good. Mother was always afraid I would catch cold, but I was really in better shape than with so many clothes on.

Our school was a one room building with a hall across the front of the building where children hung our coats and hats. Our heat was from a large stove with a heavy jacket around the outside. The teacher had to put wood in the stove for us to have heat. If it got too hot, we had to open a window. All of us had desks to sit at and of course the teacher had her large desk also. When the weather was bad outside we had to play games inside for our recess period. There were two toilets outside one for the boys and one for the girls and quite a distance for each of us to run to get there. We had a ball field outside in the back where we would play baseball and sometimes we would play dodge ball. I remember either my first or second grade, someone put pepper on top of the stove, and we all began sneezing and sneezing and finally the teacher had to stop class and figure out who did that. It turned out to be a big boy in one of the upper grades and my, but he did get a slapping. I was so glad it wasn't me.

Another time that I can remember well, is when we had a fire near the schoolhouse. There was a lady that lived near the school Mrs. Steward that decided to burn off her yard and she did and then the pasture near her house caught fire and it came up to the school. We grabbed every bucket, pan we could find and started carrying water to put all around the school yard so it wouldn't burn the school. That was an exciting time! I remember being on the handle of the cistern and turned with all my might while the others carried water. Smoke was heavy, and it gave us all a scare. Luckily, we were able to get the fire out and save the school house. My mother came to the school about the time it was all over but there was still lots of smoke and she was afraid for all of us. I think the fire did jump the road and it burned some of the woods we always went through to get to the school but on a whole we were very lucky. I was glad to see mother and have a ride home from school.

I remember how my mother would caution me not to get in the car with a stranger. You would almost hate to see a car coming as they might stop, and you would have to tell them "No Thanks!" I got a few rides but not many. There were also two creeks between Lloyd's house and mine. One had a bridge over it and the other one didn't. There was brush piled on each side of the road and in the summer time and late spring sometimes you would see snakes all entwined in the brush and that would nearly scare me to death. How could I make it across to the other side and not have a snake to chase after me...I thought they were blue racers but of course I couldn't be sure. Many times, I would run with all my might to get through that dip without something happening.

In the summertime sometimes, you would see a covered wagon pulled by two horses going through the country and occasionally we would have to pass them and the one handling the horses would give a loud noise that would make chills go up and down your spine. I remember one-time dad was in the field and mother, Jean and I were in the house and a lady with a covering over her head and a long dress came to the front door. Mother told Jean and I to stay out of sight while she went to the door and the lady wanted some medicine for her little girl who was sick. These people were known as gypsy's and you could not believe their story, so mother told her she didn't have any medicine for the sick child. The lady left, and I was so happy she did. Many times, if they had a chance they would steal things and so they couldn't be trusted. Some people would have more than one coming to your door and one would go one way and another one another way if they could slip in they would.

I liked my teacher a lot, her name was Virginia Baynum. In two years, my sister Jean, started school. There weren't very many in my class, I know of two, which were Reva McClintock and Harold Lloyd Colliver. Had a different teacher a Mrs. Ruth (Roland) Brown, for the second grade and then third and fourth grades were taught by one of my favorite teachers, Mrs. Ellen LaRue. Ethel Owen was fifth and sixth and Oleta James, for seventh and eighth, no two teachers were alike. I attended all of my eight grades in the one room school and graduated from grade school when I was thirteen years old in 1941. I always said one of my teachers was so very nice out of the school room and a bear inside the classroom. Guess we worked on her nerves----something happened.

My sister started to school in 1935 and I had to look after her and help her where needed if I could she usually had a head of her own, and really didn't want help.

LIVING LIKE EVERYONE ELSE

In 1938 I couldn't believe it, but Ralls County Electric started stringing wires and we were able to get electricity. How wonderful! I had wanted it for years. Aunt Alma and Uncle Baxter Watts had had electricity for years and now we could finally get it. What a thrill to use a switch and turn on the light! The upstairs lights were only a long wire with a bulb on the end of it. But at least it was a light. Whatever mom and dad did it was the simplest and cheapest way possible. They used regular fixtures in all of the rooms except the living room and there wasn't a ceiling light in there and again you had to carry in a lamp to have light. I never understood that one. So even though we had electricity it didn't help when you wanted to play the piano at night, I was so very disappointed. It didn't stop me practicing however.

It took a year or two for us to get a TV after the electric wiring got done. Finally, probably a year or so, we got our first TV. You would turn it on and have to wait for it to warm up. Quite different from the ones of today and the picture on TV's of today is so much better than it was then. But we were very proud we had one.

Several things were bought as time went on like an electric washer and that was nice to use. One time I caught my fingers in the wringer, not too badly, but bad enough it sure hurt but I didn't let on and they did get well.

We also got different irons to iron with and an electric iron was so nice to use. But, we still had to sprinkle down the clothes or at least most of them to get the wrinkles out.

Phones changed also and as time passed we finally got one that you dial the numbers and that was cool.

I have to tell about carrying a large lunch bucket with a thermos in the top and of course kids will get into mischief. Lloyd and I didn't always agree on things and a few times my only defense was to use the dinner bucket but never did much harm with it, but Lloyd always told such stories on how I would hit him with it, and he was so abused. Not saying what all he did to deserve it. Many times, I would be asked to come into his house and it was always such a delight as many times Aunt Alma would be baking rolls, and she would always give me one fresh one out of the oven and "My, but it was good!" I had a path down the grassy hill there and would enjoy the roll as I made my way home. Jean was just as happy to get the treat also. My mother made rolls but most of the time she was making them other times rather than just when I would get home which was the time it was wanted most, as kids are always hungry after a long and hard day at school. A few times I had dough-nuts, or maybe a cookie but most of the time it was rolls. Mother's rolls were sometimes very good and other time they weren't, I would ask why, and she finally admitted that she never measured anything so that must have been the reason. Kids want them good every time naturally, to this day I measure everything.

Nights that I didn't stop at Lloyd's and would come on home of course I was starved -- I needed something to eat and I could find nothing except a slice or two of bread and I would spread it with butter and add sugar on top of the butter. That was good, I seldom had jelly or something else to put on top. Occasionally, I would notice that one of the students had minced ham sandwiches and bought bread, I thought why couldn't I have that in my lunch at least once in a while? He also had cookies that looked so good. They were chocolate with marshmallow tops and sometimes they were other colors also. My, but that would be good to eat! Occasionally mother would buy the ham and cookies but not very often. I usually had a cold biscuit for bread with some kind of meat like sausage or something. A few times we had cookies maybe some she would make occasionally. We didn't have much fruit to eat either, when carrying our lunch.

I was told to never get in the car with anyone we didn't know. Sometimes I was always hoping that they wouldn't even stop and ask. It seemed that mother was afraid of a lot of little things. You couldn't go wading in the creek, and go visiting without asking, and the list goes on and on. Couldn't go to Lloyd's unless I asked first. Couldn't ride horses. Sometimes I felt it was endless of the things I couldn't do.

When some of the kids had birthdays, the mothers would bring cookies for all of the kids and that was a wonderful treat. I know that Mrs. Calhoun would come many times around Valentine's Day and would bring a large box of cookies all decorated. What fun and were they good! In the fall we would have a pie supper after a program, that the students had a part in. Each pupil would bring a box, or a pie and they would be auctioned off at the end of the program. This was how we made money for the school and sometimes people would run the price of a box up on certain people. It was sort of a fun night and lots of excitement. The teacher and students worked mighty hard to get ready for that night of putting on the program of songs, plays and poems. It was hard to relax in front of people and do your part. As you grew older you couldn't help but wonder who would buy your box but most of the time nothing too exciting happened.

One year I think it was the third and fourth grade, the teacher had a rhythm band and crepe paper uniform. The boys really hated the crepe paper uniforms, they thought they were sissy looking. Our instruments were drums, sticks, cymbals and bells. We usually had the teacher to play the piano or had a victrola to be played so we could follow along. Either the teacher or a student would be the director.

During the summer months and fall sometimes Aunt Alma would like someone to gather beans, peas and sometimes grapes. I thought that was fun and enjoyed helping her out when she had lots to do. Many times, she would give me a quarter or two and I was so happy about that. I never knew what it was to get money for doing anything before.

A family by the name of Herron lived across the pasture. I was over there one time, I think with dad and they invited me into their house. They had an old piano that had a player, that you had to pump the pedals with your feet to get it to play the rolls of music, that were put in place above the keyboard. That was very fascinating to me to put a roll of paper with holes in it in place and work the pedals and music would come out of an instrument. How could that be? I was able to go a few times before the family moved away and was so happy about that. Dad bought the place across the road from the Watts place after renting it a few years and then finally tore the house down.

During the summer someone would have a larger dinner sort of like a family reunion at one of my aunts and that was always fun to look forward to. Maybe one or two of my aunts would be visiting from Rock Island and Moline, Illinois as Aunt Etra and Aunt Lillian lived there. Of all of the food that was fixed you had lots to eat, and so many kids to play with it was great fun! I would wonder why we didn't have a dinner and invite everyone, but we didn't. Mother seemed to think she had enough to do without all of that company and she let the others have the dinners. Once in a while later on, Uncle Leo and Aunt Una Hager would visit and stay a night or two. Dad also had two sister's that lived in Oakwood that married Gibbons, Iona married Noah and Lera married Otis, we called him Uncle Oat. Iona had five girls and Lera had ten children. Guess I'll tell this now, she lived to be 99 and had worked hard all of her life. I said then, "that children and hard work doesn't kill you, it is everything else." Just a little joke that goes with the family – One day she needed soda for making some biscuits, and so sent one of her children to the store. The store keeper said, 'Do you want the liquid or dry?' The child answered, 'Oh just give me the liquid' and so they did. When the child arrived home and gave the bottle to mother she said, 'I can't make biscuits with that!' So, the joke lives on, you think they know, but they don't.

Aunt Iona worked hard also, and we didn't see them very much it seemed. I remember hearing she did ironing for people and that is hard work. When the girls were living we would maybe see them once a year but not very often. They seemed to sort of stay to themselves.

Mother was always telling the stories of how she used to ride horses. I had heard it for years. She said, she always got permission from her dad, and he would say yes, and she would ride. Evidently, she spent many days riding but when I would ask if I could ride she would say NO! So Lloyd and I had a talk about riding, and I thought of the idea that our fathers were over at the Herron place across the road from my house, with the team of horses doing some work, and I thought it would be fun for both of us to go over there and when they started home we would ask if we could ride on the horses with the harness on. Mother gave the okay for us to go and find our dad's. But when we arrived home and riding on the horses and our dad's walking along side of us you should have heard "My Mother!" She threw a fit!! We had asked our dad's and they had said okay, and were walking beside us and she disapproved? I couldn't believe it, but it was true.

SOME PLEASURES FOR EVERYONE

Every fall we would start having card parties. We would invite enough people in the neighborhood to have four or five tables. You would draw for partners the men against the women and the fun would start. They would gather probably about five thirty and the party would begin. At first, they had full meals and then play cards and other times you would play awhile and then eat and play some more. This was for adults only and I was always one of the helpers to get everything fixed, food, tables and etc. The tables would all have white tablecloths and napkins on them and everything just so. I seem to remember fixing sandwiches of two different kinds and then salads and desserts besides the drinks which was usually tea and coffee. This was quite a thing and you always hoped it went well. We spent hours getting ready for this. Some of the people playing cards had done this for years and I remember one particular incident of a couple that usually came together, and this time only Fred came. We asked what happened to Oza and he looked funny and said "Oh, I left her holding the gate, and I had better go get her." Later on, Oza came and didn't say a word about anything. Fred came later and said, "She passed me up in the "Old Pickup Truck" and didn't even stop," we all laughed and laughed the rest of the evening. A funny thing that happened and you don't forget this one. Just one of many! Everyone took turns having a party and that made a fun time for everyone. Prizes were given away for the lady and gentleman that had the highest and lowest scores. Sometimes I had to fill in if a player was sick or something, and I would play. I would be so scared if I had to play with my dad, as he didn't want you to make a mistake, and took everything very seriously and would scold me if I didn't play right. Card games went on through my schooling and even after I married.

I started to high school in 1941. I thought it would be such a thrill to get to ride a bus to school. I really wanted to go to high school in Monroe City but didn't get to. I remember the man coming to see us about what school I attended but my wants didn't help, I was made to go to Center. I didn't think that mother even talked like she was wanting us to go to Monroe City, but what I said, did little good. Lloyd's sisters, Mary Sue and Dorothy attended week-ends. I tried to make mother understand I was big enough to stay in an apartment, but she didn't think so. She was always very protective of me.

Center was a smaller school and many times by the time I was to take a subject it was not offered or done without a teacher. For instance, I wanted to take typing and that year they didn't have a commerce teacher, so I had to take it. You would read about the machine and then press a lever and see what happens. I was determined to go by the directions and try to do it like it was supposed to be done and very thankful that I did, as a result I can still type and do well. Our supervisor was the Methodist minister. I made a good grade but was not the fastest typist. I chose classes each year, so I could graduate and did in 1945 at the age of sixteen. I was next to the youngest in the entire class. Most of the students were six when they started. I wondered if my education would be as good as it would if I went to Monroe City.

I still had to walk over to Lloyd's house in order to catch the bus, it never did come to my door or driveway. I wouldn't have known how it felt to have one come to the door. Latin was another class I took, and I really enjoyed the subject and during the year I had three teachers and finally the year ended, and I was only half way through the book. That was really too bad as I enjoyed the class and had not learned enough. How I wished I had gone to Monroe City to school, I am sure you didn't have this to contend with. Things were not right in the school system at Center.

There were many basketball games during high school and how I was always wishing I could go and whenever something was going on that I wanted to attend I would start asking my parents if they would take me. They seemed to enjoy the basketball games, and so I did get to attend a lot of them especially if it was the tournaments in Center. Whenever something was on I would start begging to attend and most of the time it worked but occasionally it didn't.

I remember one spring there was a track meet some place and someone was driving a truck and a large group of us went in the back of the truck to the track meet. I got sun and wind burned so bad my face pealed and sore it was terrible! I didn't do that anymore---I would rather stay most anyplace rather than have that to happen.

I remember the year 1941, standing in the bedroom at home and we had the radio on, and the announcement from President Roosevelt that, "World War II was declared." That statement gave you a jolt. War was going on all through

High School and when I graduated there were only sixteen of us as two were in the service. War ended in September 1945, the year I graduated. The service guys were Willis Walker and Bradford Hulse. Brad turned out to be my brother-in-law. He married my sister Jean in 1948.

We sometimes went to a movie as a family but only certain ones that mother and dad would enjoy. I remember one that we saw was "Gone With The Wind" but unless a real popular one the answer was NO!

I had some special girlfriends that I so enjoyed and got to visit them every once in a while. Some people took basketball but I didn't as my folks would not like the trips for practice and so I declined.

Life in high school was a challenge. I knew that if I did get asked for a date, I had to decline, as mother had told me I couldn't date. I was with a mixed group a few times but never a single date. One of my friends, that was a senior in high school went into the service and we wrote back and forth for several years. He sent me some nice gifts and one time a horned toad. That was an experience, but it lived several years.

Occasionally dad would come home with a new car and didn't even know that he was thinking of doing anything like that. Many times, you wondered if he had moved everything out of the old car, but he always said yes, and shrugged his shoulders and on he would go. If he didn't that is just the way it was.

When I started to high school was when the war started, and people were buying bonds. Time and time again dad would give me a thousand dollar check for me to buy a bond. This went on several weeks until I had bought ten bonds. I was amazed and said to dad, "I thought we didn't have any money," and he shrugged his shoulders and said, "I have a little!" Dad knew that by making do and doing without he would save a little money and that is what he did and worked very hard. A good lesson to learn for everyone both then and now.

Several summers we organized 4-H groups and I worked on sewing and woodworking. I really enjoyed doing that and a way to learn to do things. How I wished I had my own sewing machine but that didn't happen either. We also learned to get along with others and worked together doing our projects. Learning to be a leader and doing your work well. Mother wouldn't hardly let me touch her sewing machine as she said, "I would get it out of kilter."

In other words, she thought I would get it to where it wouldn't sew, so she didn't want me to touch it. That made it hard to learn something if she didn't trust me. Seemed to me I did a few articles in sewing such as hemming a tea towel and making an apron, not sure on anything else. I did some nice projects in woodworking such as a sewing cabinet, book ends and a pair of lawn chairs that I still have.

All of the classes would have skating parties, where you would go to Hannibal and roller skate. How I would love to do that and again, I would start on my parents early, so as to maybe get to go. I was never a good skater but sure did love trying, and so much fun to be with the group. Sometimes they would go on the bus and some way I would be able to go but not very often. One time I talked my parents into having a hay ride for a large group of kids and dad did say yes to that, think we roasted hot dogs and marshmallows afterwards which was so much fun

At school, in Center, you many times wondered what to do with yourself except talk to your friends after lunch. Well, there was a piano on the stage and many times i would sit down to play and a group would gather around, and I would play some pieces I would think of and then others would ask me to play a certain piece and it went on and on. If someone would sing the tune of the piece I could usually play it. A very enjoyable time for all. We all wondered how I did it and so did I, with God's help I was able to do it.

They did have a movie place in Center and a place where you could dance by the record player which was fun. Something you could do, a few times I rode with Lloyd there but think he had trouble getting to do things also. I was told I couldn't go on a date until I was sixteen so another rule that seemed unfair but had to abide by. I know that my sister wasn't supposed to be dating with others, but she seemed to work it with friends and did lots of things she wasn't supposed to do by spending the night with her friends and dating and etc. The bus was always stopping at Lane's store for kids to buy things and I never had any money, but my sister seemed to always have some, and she had taken it out of the drawers at home and spent it however she wanted especially for candy. She seemed to always get by with whatever she decided to do.

I would watch for times that Dorothy, Lloyd's sister would come home sometimes she had time to go to the creek with Lloyd and I otherwise, I couldn't go. She was a lot of fun and we enjoyed every minute of it. She was a school teacher and spent her week ends with her folks. Mary Sue was older, and she went to Quincy, IL to be a nurse and did her training there also. She began dating a guy from Pittsfield, IL and later married this guy who was Gordon Batley. He was such a nice man and so much fun to be around.

The summers found people putting up bundles of wheat and I knew that a guy that I liked the looks of would be working there. I had two of my aunts which were Dad's sister's the Bixler's and Hager's would be fixing big dinners for the hay crew, and if I could talk mother into going out there and helping them, maybe I could see Ivan, a guy that seemed to be a heart throb for me. Of course, I didn't let on for that reason except my Aunt Angella and Aunt Una really needed help. We did go a few times and I got to pour Ivan a glass of tea or whatever he was drinking. What a thrill!!! I thought he was such a nice-looking guy, blonde, blue eyed and strong built man.

As the years passed the phone service did get a little better. The looks of the phone changed and finally went to rotary phones and that was quite an improvement. I think we still had 4 or 6 people on the line and that was a challenge too. We didn't hear but one phone ring and that part was good.

One summer I was trying to learn to ride Lloyd's bicycle which was really not easy. I always wished for a bike but that was a NO, NO so it was ride Lloyd's -- it was my only chance to learn. He let me borrow it for a few days and was doing fine, and my sister decided to take it down the incline into the basement. She said she was only walking it down the incline and fell after getting into the basement and hit her wrist against the cement that was around the chimney. I was sure she rode it down the incline, but she said "No!" at the time. Years later, she finally confessed and laughed about it -- I didn't think that was funny, but she did.

When I was sixteen and a senior I was able to get my driver's license by going into a business in Center, MO., which looked sort of like a car place with various things that you might need for a car. I just simply told them that I wanted my driver's license and they filled out a paper for me and asked for a quarter. That is all it cost, and no questions asked. So easy but you sure couldn't do that now. I was so very proud of that I was beaming but when it came to driving that was a different story and I was told so many times that I couldn't drive that I even said than "Why did I spend my quarter for my license if I can't drive?" My folks were afraid I would wreck the car and then they wouldn't have a car to go in. That would have been terrible! Some way I needed to learn and needed help from someone. I was finally showed a little bit about the car but only two or three times and that was it.

WHAT DO I DO NOW?

Such is life, I was told I couldn't go to work anywhere and I was determined not to just stay home and keep house. Mother wanted me to just stay home and work there and I was determined I was going to do something not just stay home. I had thought of being a beauty operator or a teacher. They wouldn't let me go to Hannibal and stay there for schooling for a beauty operator. Another thing I thought of was to go to Hannibal, as I had heard that Eva Mae Yager, one of my classmates, was there and had a job at the telephone office. I thought that would be great, but I was told I could not go to Hannibal and stay and work and room with Eva. You would have thought I was a bad girl and not a chance of doing much of anything. So, dad finally said he would pay for me to attend Hannibal LaGrange College. I wasn't long deciding to do that, and I stayed in the girl's dorm. Mother told me, "if I didn't come home every week end I didn't love her, so every week end I had to pack up my things and come home. It was very hard to meet friends and have fun if you had to come home. I missed so much at college, when you had to be home every week end. A few times, maybe two or three weekends I stayed there but the rest I came home to please my parents. I had a health problem as well as just didn't know how to study so in January I quit and stayed home the next semester. I was really sorry I did that, and my I was determined that I was going back and finish, as I was tired of spending my time cleaning the house and doing all of the tasks that needed to be done. My sister was there but she could have cared less about whether things were clean or not. Not a worry in the world about things! She had two more years of high school left. I am sure she had dates because she was always going to a friend's house and spending the night and I heard little things about what she was doing but that didn't matter it seemed.

One of the highlights in college the first semester was to be selected as Daisy Mae. We had this contest and I remember getting my outfit together and had to do with what I had. I found an old Navy-blue skirt and made the bottom of it real ragged. The top I could not think of any polka dot material that I had so I took an old pillow slip and made it into a blouse and used red cake coloring for the dots on the blouse. I looked at her picture and tried to get my hair to look like Daisy and "I Got It!" I was surprised, but happy. I have forgotten who Lil Abner was, but guess it doesn't matter.

I tried to be in several things in college like the Trojanettes, Future Teachers of America, and the Young Women's Missionary Society of the Southern Baptist Convention. I also will never forget the time I was asked to pray at a meeting and I had never done that before out loud and my thoughts were "God Help Me!" He did, and I was able to do this and that made me so happy. Now it is easier to pray aloud but that particular time I was scared half to death.

I did date a few guys at HLG but no one steady. One time we were at the Huntington Christian Church at an ice cream supper a guy that I knew, Ivan Lehenbauer, asked me to eat with him. I was thrilled, and I was hoping he would ask me for more dates but had no idea whether he would or not. I knew he had been dating another gal and you never know what is really going on. Maybe I was more anxious than he. You never know about the guys. Ha!! He would ask me every few weeks for a date---he said later, he wanted me to date others if I wanted to. He wanted to give me time to do that. Nice, but a little different, of course he was busy with farming also.

Another thing that I thought was a little unusual was that Ivan's mother was a sister to dad's sister's husband Albert Bixler. So, we would have the same aunt and uncle if we married, which was, a little unusual. Two of dad's sisters lived a half mile apart south and west of here and were very good cooks. Each one was always trying to outdo the other in a happy way. Aunt Angelia had one girl and Aunt Una had none, she was married to Leo Hager.

My dad had bought a new John Deere tractor to farm with and of course he wouldn't let me drive that either. Lloyd wanted his dad to buy a tractor and he wouldn't do it, he would only farm with horses and so Lloyd decided to join the army. I hated to see him go but we were both hurt with our parents being the way they were.

By the next September I was more than ready to go back to HLG to school and I stayed until spring of that year. I hadn't gotten into the year very long when Lloyd came home from the service. He had joined the Army Air Corp, because his dad would not buy a tractor. He thought if Uncle Willie could have a tractor, so could his dad, which was very true.

He was home on furlough when he asked me to bring someone home with me that was tall, thin, and you know what I mean. I said okay, and asked Mildred Whitley if she would like to come home with me and go out on a blind date? She said, "she didn't have anything better to do," and did just that. She came home with me and I introduced her to Lloyd and they were a match and I was happy about that. Usually Lloyd's thoughts were the same as mine and he wanted a date and it worked.

I took music and art courses and really enjoyed them and one of my basic courses was Practice Teaching and was led by Dorothy Prince, that was Dr. Prince's daughter. That was so good, and she was such a lovely person I enjoyed every minute of it. This was first grade at Mark Twain grade school, a truly wonderful course and teacher.

How I hated to see the ones that I had started with graduating from college and I had stayed out that semester and now I was behind. This was only a two-year college. As a result, I had to attend two summers to make up for the semester I stayed home. Mother and Dad still wouldn't buy me any kind of a car and so I had to be taken everywhere I went. The last summer I rode back and forth with a friend, Lula Thompson and that was doubly hard for I needed help with a math course and when you rode back and forth with someone else you didn't have time for help from anyone.

I remember the second year when I started back probably the second semester the matron, Miss Bena and I became real good friends. She found out that I had a Ouija board and she had a male friend that she was hoping he would ask her for a date, so she wanted me to come downstairs after hours and we would work the Ouija board. I did, and we had lots of laughs over the answers. For those that don't know what a Ouija board is, it is a board that you place your fingers on and I think it is the electricity in your body that moves the board going to different letters. It is funny and mysterious but just like anything else it might be true, and it might not. Only God knows on that and many other things. Haven't been able to get anyone to work the board with me since, not even my grandkids. How about that!!!

My sister Jean announced that she and Brad Hulse were going to get married and they with my folks went to Hannibal and were married in the minister's home, June 27, 1948. Seemed strange but that's the way it happened, and I wasn't asked to attend or anything. It suddenly happened and that was that. Jean and Brad started housekeeping near Center, MO. Not much was said over that, whatever she wanted to do she did.

Mother wouldn't even let me stay by myself on weekends while they went to Monroe shopping, she was afraid something would happen to me no matter how old I was. GEE!!! After a full year and one summer I got a job at Center grade school as a teacher of grades third and fourth. I did have to take an exam to be a teacher as I didn't have my 60 plus hours to be a teacher, I had all of the requirements but not enough electives to graduate. I took the exam and passed, and I was thrilled. I got an apartment with two other teachers, Faye Dixon, who was dating and married Dr. Prince, and Elsie Baker who married Jack Jones. We had a big stove that heated the apartment and one day I was having a problem with the stove and getting it to burn and I used a little kerosene to get it started and it went "Poof!" and blew soot, burnt my eyebrows, singed my hair and I smelled like a singed chicken all day. "Wasn't that great!!" I'll never forget that day for sure. I enjoyed living with the two gals and thought we would do that again another year. Found that Faye decided to get married and not come back and Elsie made it up with another teacher to move and room with her and that left me all alone in the apartment. That didn't set so well so I gave up the apartment and moved elsewhere. It took a while to get over that deal as hard to forget. However, I did find an upstairs room to rent for the next year in a private home.

The two younger Neuschafer kids took music lessons from me my second-year teaching and it was an enjoyable time for all.

My folks did let me take the car two times to Center for one night and otherwise to come home I had to ride the school bus and walk home carrying my suitcase. My thoughts were, "When will they ever trust me to do anything?"

I taught for a total of two years and was dating a guy by the name of Ivan Lehenbauer. The same one I had poured tea for at the time they were threshing wheat.

WEDDING PLANS

We decided to get married in August and I had thought I would continue to teach but Ivan didn't want me to, so I didn't. I sure hated to give up what I had longed to do but decided to please him and not continue. I thought living with his mother and brother would let me do it and he still wouldn't starve. Ha!

In June while we were deciding about our wedding plans we got an invitation to Lloyd and Mildred's wedding in St Louis at Scott Air Force Base. We were able to go and attend the wedding and reception. That was very nice. a very, happy time together. They were going to be living at different places as Lloyd being in the service, he wasn't for sure where he might be going.

I talked to my parents about getting married, and was told I could get married, but not married in a church. Dad said, "Church weddings were for show, and we didn't need that." I disagreed, but no changing him for sure. I could tell that something was not right about me marrying Ivan, and I asked my parents, "What is Wrong? Do you not want me to marry Ivan, do you have something against the man? Dad said finally, "He is a republican." I said, "Is that all you have against him?" No answer, "I couldn't believe my ears!" Ivan never talked politics and so that didn't enter my mind. Maybe the Lehenbauer family was mainly republican, but so what! I said, "If that is all you have against him, I'm marrying him in a way, I love him."

We were married in my home, where I was born and raised and called the Watts Homestead, by a friend that I went to Hannibal- LaGrange with, a ministerial student, Homer Arendall, who was married to my best friend, Jewel. Ivan's brother Bennie and my sister, Jean stood up with us. We had a quiet ceremony, in my living room. After a few pictures we had some cake and punch and a change of clothes, we were off on our honeymoon. I had to get married in a navy-blue dress and that is because you couldn't find a white dress in Hannibal, not even white material. It was too far, so my folks thought, to go to Quincy or anywhere else to get another dress. I was really upset but did no good. Jean had the white dress on that she got married in the summer before and she wouldn't wear anything else. That was just something, I had to accept even though it was very hard. I had made my going away suit and I was proud of that, I had bought myself a sewing machine, so mother could not say anything as she was always telling me I couldn't sew on her machine I would mess the working of the machine in some way. Unbelievable!! We headed out on our honeymoon and our plans were to go west. I knew that it was almost silo time, so we had to get a trip in, or we wouldn't have one. I definitely wanted us to have some time together as we were going to live with his mother and brother. I wanted some private time together and I was determined to have it.

Lloyd and Mildred Watts were stationed in Cheyenne, Wyoming and I thought it would be nice to go by and surprise them. Our plans were to head that way and since I had their address, we were able to find their basement apartment and had it all planned. When I got to the top of the steps, Ivan said something to me. I answered him, and Lloyd looked at Mildred and said, "There's Wanda!" Gee!! I couldn't even surprise them!! We had a good time nevertheless, they had gotten married in June just before Ivan and I did in August. We spent a short time with them and then on to the Yellowstone Park and other places of interest. We were gone most of two weeks.

When we got home I couldn't help but think about a group of friends and neighbors might give us a chivalry. This is when they would gather outside the home or place where the bride and groom lived. They would make lots of noise until the bride and groom come outside and then the noise would stop. Everyone visits, and drinks such as soda and beer would be given out to the crowd. I knew that Ivan had done so many things to chivalry other's, it was hard telling what they might do to us. I have heard of them wheeling the couple in wheelbarrows dumping them in the pond and etc. I was sort of scared, when you think about it. Thank goodness, nothing like that happened, and I was thrilled. I never noticed anyone going inside but when we went upstairs to go to bed we had rocks all under the covers. We had a laugh over that, as the mess had to be cleaned up before we could lie down and rest. That took a while after finding a bucket to put them in.

We both had lots of things to do. I know I asked Ivan, what he liked to eat? He said, "bread, meat and potatoes." I said, "what about vegetables and salads and he wasn't for sure about those." We started having them nevertheless. Life here was very busy! We had a yard full of shrubs and etc. Cattle to take care of, as well as hogs, chickens, and guineas. I couldn't help but wonder how things would go when I was actually in a home that someone else was in charge. How could we manage? We did manage and got along. It wasn't exactly easy, and I had hoped that sometime soon we would have our own place, but that was the question! We had a wood stove to cook on winter and summer on the west wall of the kitchen, a metal sink cabinet on the south side of the kitchen, and a large cabinet on the north that held the dishes and it was called the "old press". Our table and wood box were on the east. In fact, "the whole house was heated by stoves." By spring I asked, "can't we do something to this kitchen, and make it a little more handy to do things?" I didn't want to spend a lot of money but just do something. We ended up ordering kitchen cabinets from Sears and putting them together and we really worked over the kitchen making it more handy than we had it before and doing way more than I had anticipated. We had cabinets to put dishes in without walking so far to put them away. We also bought another stove and that made such a difference in the cooking especially in the summertime. Before getting the other stove, I would have dinner all on cooking, and be so happy about that, when I would remember, "Oh gee, I forgot to put wood in the stove!" Sometimes that made it very bad for dinner—especially if I was baking something. I would blame things on the wood stove, if they didn't turn out well when it might have been my fault, for letting the fire die down or I didn't do the mixing right.

We also decided to make the pantry into a bathroom and that was great to say the least. The outhouse they had was so very large and had big rocks that you had to step on to get inside. I thought after I married, I sure didn't better myself when it came to the bathroom, as they didn't have one here. They did have water in the house at the kitchen sink and electricity. The county line between Marion and Ralls is the highway and we own land running up to the highway. Years ago, Ralls County wanted the Lehenbauer's to pay for every pole coming from the south, eight tenths of a mile and Marion would bring the poles in from the highway seven tenths of a mile and no charge. As a result, the Lehenbauer's chose Marion County over Ralls, which was a very good decision as their electricity is so much cheaper than Ralls. They don't charge to do jobs on the electricity usually in Marion County. I always say that Ralls charges for them to bend over.

The living room was heated with an oil stove and registers were cut in the floor to let heat come upstairs to where our bedroom was. That heated Virgil's room also and his mother room was downstairs.

Ivan's mother was not a person doing anything fancy. She was as plain as could be, but clean. I immediately thought I would like to put some ruffled curtains up to the upstairs windows in our bedroom. Very soon I went to Hannibal and bought the material and made them. I was so very proud I was able to do that. Think they were the first curtains I had ever made. Ivan and I purchased a new three-piece bedroom suite for the room as there was no storage place for clothes. A very small closet and that was it. There were two bedrooms upstairs and one downstairs where his mother stayed, and Virgil having the other one upstairs.

LEARNING NEW THINGS AND BUILDING OUR HOME

By fall of this year there was talk of extension clubs and I thought it would be a great thing to have in Huntington as I was a new bride and did not know a lot about cooking, canning and things about sewing, decorating homes and etc. So, I was instrumental in starting the club in the area called the Huntington Homemakers. Mrs. L. L. Houchins and Miss Hepler the Home Demonstration Agent of Ralls County came to meet with the group at the home of Mrs. W. D. Lehenbauer, (Nora Lee). They insisted that I be president; vice president, Mrs. Grover Vail; and secretary and treasurer; Mrs. Emmett Smith. We had several ladies of the community to be in our club. I thought we did well and lasted for a number of years. Ralls had a great Extension group of people. All sorts of things were taught.

That first spring we decided to have some chickens to raise and we went over to Perry to get them and came home with 500 chickens. My thoughts were, "What have I gotten myself into?" To go for 200 or maybe 250 and come home with 500, unbelievable! We made it with all of them and dressed chickens that spring and that was a job to say the least. I was so happy when they were taken care of. I didn't want to do that again.

One day I decided to make bread. I had never done that before and so I had a recipe and started out and I got in a sticky mess it was terrible! I had flour on the floor, cabinet and dough all over my hands and some of my utensils. I tried and tried to work flour into the dough and it only got to be more of a mess rather than better. I had never had anything like that to happen. I had added the flour that it said, and it was still so sticky, I was ready to go throw it over the fence, bowl and all, when his mother came to my rescue and patiently added more and more flour until it was under control. My patience was gone!

I don't remember how the bread or rolls tasted but it was a long time before trying another recipe. I kept trying recipes until I found one that I could control, and things started working well after that. I now love to make bread and tea rings.

Just south of here probably a mile lived Ed and Mate Lehenbauer, Ivan's, first cousin. They had twin boys and prior to them they had a daughter that was deceased. Maurice married a gal in Monroe City, Naomi Hill and Marvin married Lois Wilson from Hannibal. Maurice lived in Monroe City and Marvin and Lois decided to build a house near his parents and live there. We were very close and did many things together. Both Marvin and Maurice worked at the rock quarry called Central Stone. They were there when it first opened up, and to this day it is still blasting and crushing rock for people. This road has a lot of big trucks on it hauling rock. One time they measured how many trucks and there were over seven hundred trucks on this road in one day's time. Lois worked at the shoe factory in Hannibal and Naomi was a beauty operator.

We always wished we could have more water and had to have water hauled many times. So, we decided to drill for water. We even had a person that witches for water come and we drilled right where he told us to drill but hit only hard rock and even though we drilled through that, still "No Water." We drilled three holes and didn't get water at all. It was very discouraging. We knew if we built a house, we had to haul water for the foundation and basement area.

People found out that I could play the piano and asked me to give their kids piano lessons. For a while I went to the Huntington school and gave lessons in the old Huntington School, as I didn't have a piano. A little awkward but the children were eager to learn and that worked for a while. I think at that time I had three students.

Thinking we lived in a quiet neighborhood and not too much going on. Of course, in Huntington there were, two stores, a post office in one of the stores, and railroad tracks. Across from one of the stores that was owned by the Warren brothers was where they Warren's lived. This happened to be the house that was where my grandparents lived, Mr. and Mrs. John R. Baxter, the parents of Mary Catherine Baxter who married John R Watts, my great-grandparents.

While working here on the farm we felt very secure, and of course we were very busy here. One morning I think it was 1953. The news in the area was there had been two murders just north and a little east out near the highway. What a shock to hear that! We knew nothing about it. The news was that Hubert Jones who lived near the highway just east of the road by our house and on the north side of the highway was found dead in the barn. It was told that he had been having parties in the barn, and he was found dead on the hay. Than just down the road on the opposite side the highway a body of a guy, by the name of Chisham was found in a feed trough with a gun at his side. They said he shot himself, but the thoughts were that he didn't, as the body was lying very straight in the trough. If he had fired the gun he would not have been in that position. GEE!! Who did it? They didn't seem to do much investigating. At least we didn't hear of very much done. The question was, "Who did the two murders?" And no one knew the answer. I don't think they even had a trial or anything. I know that Rayford and Josephine Straub bought the Jones place and was told they had to send the money to England to pay for it. A very strange thing to happen, and no real answers. This was never solved, the Chisham guy was one of the boys whose father delivered ice to my house when I was a little girl, small world, isn't it?

There were two houses one across the road from the other and were owned by Charlie Meeker. Ralph Adams lived on the south side of the highway and his parents lived on the other. Ralph and Wilma had two little girls and we spent quite a bit of time together as Ralph loved to go coon hunting, and Wilma and I enjoyed each other's company. When the guys would go hunting Wilma and I would plan something. Sometimes I would take my crocheting and spend time doing that while Wilma many times made dresses for the girls. I think they were about three and probably five. Ralph's parents were Sam and Fountie Adams.

After years of marriage we decided to build a house. Before building I said, we had to make sure the farm was ours, Ivan's and mine. We could not build a house without first paying off everyone, so it was ours, I begged for it to be our house, and build it in the pasture, south of the old house. but Ivan just wouldn't agree. This is tearing his mother's house down, actually it was where Virgil, Ivan's older brother lived also. We could keep it standing and be close enough to take care of them when they needed it. Ivan thought the house needed to come down and he wanted his mother and brother to experience the new house also. The old house had three porches besides a screened in porch across the back. The house also had a rock foundation and a small cellar underneath. I also tried to convince Ivan that we needed to build a house with more than three bedrooms and he didn't agree saying that, "They wouldn't live always," and I said, "Who says when they are going to die!" That's a terrible thought!

Ivan and I spent lots of time looking at plans with Scott Conway. I wanted to build a house we could have special quarters for his mother and Virgil, but Ivan didn't want to. I also wanted a garage on the house and he said, "absolutely not." My question was, "Why?" He said, "it can cause fires!" I was shocked and said, "There are certainly lots of people that are likely to have fires if a garage causes that." I thought that would be so much nicer than going in the back to the shed to get our car. Nevertheless, I had to give in, no changing his mind. He always said, "The Watts family were so stubborn," I laughed and said "Not anymore stubborn than the Lehenbauer's"

The business part got done, plans were drawn and on March 16, 1954, we moved things into the garage which was a shed we built in the back, where the furniture went except the overstuffed couch and things like that that went to my parents and to his brother's, Bennie and Julia's. Ivan's mother was to stay at Bennie's while we built the house also. I can't remember where Virgil went but think he was mainly in a building north of the house or at Bennie's. The weather was so very nice and warm, we thought spring was here when we started tearing up the place.

They started tearing the old house down except the kitchen, bathroom and back porch. That was left so I could cook, use the bathroom and we had a deep freeze on the back porch. This was a Maytag freezer and is still running in the basement. I cooked the meals for the people that worked on the house. Quite an experience but it worked out fine. I was glad to have that part of the house to use away from all of the tear up.

Those working on the house were mainly Lehenbauer's. Fred, Ed and Bennie (Ivan's brother) and of course Ivan. For some reason they decided to mix the cement by hand, gravel and water were also hauled. That was quite an operation, but they worked well together and got the job done. Think the basement filled with water and that was a real mess, but they got that taken care of also.

Temperature changed, and the weather got cold and four nights I refused to stay in the garage. Lois and Marvin Lehenbauer who lived about a half mile away had offered us a place to stay and those four nights we went up there as it was so cold I couldn't take it. We had a stove in there, and I could not tell the stove or Ivan were in the building.

After digging the basement in order to have the cement poured, we had to haul water and gravel and four or five men mixed and poured the cement by hand. We were told we must lay tile at the outside of the basement floor and put gravel over it and Ivan didn't want to, so he didn't. We had about four people working on the house and Bennie's wife, Julia and I did all of the woodwork in the house and that was endless, with three coats of varnish and sanding in between. Mercy!! It would be late when I went to bed for, I would clean up after the men and then have to get up the next morning at 4:30 or 5:00 and go at it again. My, but I was tired! We had our walls to be plaster and color put in the plaster, so they didn't have to be painted. Well, it got so warm that the color didn't do well and was darker in some areas than it was in others, so not a good thing. Temperatures got so warm the crops and garden didn't do well. One day it was 114 degrees and that is hot! We felt that God knew we didn't have time for a garden however you always hate for it to burn up and it was doing just that. We ran big fans to move the air, so the plaster would dry which helped but it wasn't like it should have been, but we made it and let it go. Color was put in the plaster and because of the temperature being so hot the color was not all looking the same having dark spots here and there. We wanted to get done. I lost so much weight I had a friend that told me to be sure and eat a bite of bread, between each bite of vegetables and that I must not lose any more weight. I did make it okay and felt like celebrating when we got through. The kitchen cabinets that we had installed a few years ago were put in my new kitchen and the bathroom fixtures were installed also in the new house. It sure made you feel good to see things coming together as a few months seemed like years to those of us working. I had hardwood floors throughout the house and they all had to be finished and polished except for the kitchen and bathroom floors. Ivan didn't want the basement finished even though I felt it sure would be nice. We had no spare bedrooms for visitors except the couches and that was it.

We were able to move into the house by June 16, of that year and it was finished except the back room as we built so close to the kitchen wall that you could step from one to the other. We moved in and finished adding the room on to the back. Being short of water I continued to do my laundry in the basement as I had a wringer washer and felt it used less water than an automatic washer would.

We hadn't been in the house very long when Ivan said, "I want you to go buy a piano." I couldn't believe my ears, my response was, "We just finished building a house, I don't want to buy a piano now!" His reply was, "I'm tired of you going to the Huntington school giving piano lessons, you must buy a piano." I was floored but said okay, I will. I looked at quite a few piano's and finally decided on a Baldwin Acrosonic. I kept plunking on pianos until I found one that the tone sounded right. There's a lot of differences in piano's and some due to the length of the strings, sound so much better than others. I've been very proud of my purchase and very happy. I play on it most every day. What a joy to have it!

Dad had a brother that became an engineer, that run a train so many places and when I was in town with mother and dad and we would hear a train I thought of Uncle Lonely. You didn't see him much but if you heard the train whistle and saw a man steering the train with a cigar, you could bet it was my Uncle Lonely. He was a nice-looking man, tall and with dark hair. We would run to be outside and wave to the engineer as they traveled through Monroe City. Sometimes he would even slow down, to make the trip across main street. Through all of the years growing up we never got to go there but once to see him and Aunt Frances in their home in Brookfield, MO. I always wondered why, but I wondered about lots of things and never really got an answer. When we did go I remember that Wade, Charles and David were in their teens and Wade the oldest a little younger than I. For some reason David didn't live with his parents and stayed with a couple known as the Wade's. Never did know the exact answer to that one. Once in a while Aunt Frances would come see some of the Watts's but only occasionally. She was close to Aunt Angelia and introduced Angelia and Albert Bixler's, daughter Juanita to a guy by the name of Floyd Cunningham, and years later they married. She also attended several family reunions, in the different homes of the Watts girls, and a few reunions when held in the different parks.

DEATH, ORGANIST AND BABY

The year 1955, we got the news that Lonely was dead and that was tragic news to say the least. Later we learned from family that he died of pancreatic cancer, which is a bad thing to have. Think the family kept the news sort of secret, but suddenly we had lost him. Not sure how many attended, but I don't think my family went but, not sure. Surely someone attended, but I can't seem to remember exactly who. I didn't know until later what he died of. Wade, his older son told me he died of pancreatic cancer, another with cancer.

Sunday May 5, 1957, I played the piano at Monroe City Christian church. That was the year that there was a fire and it had burnt some of the organ parts. The organist Edna Boulware wanted to be gone so I was asked to play.

Our first child was born in Hannibal, MO. on May 9, 1957. She was a little girl weighing only 4 lb. and 6 oz. She was born with a hair lip and cleft and was sent immediately to St Louis Children's Hospital where she stayed for nineteen days. Doctors immediately fixed her lip. I didn't see her until the 19th of May, and when the doctor said, "You can bring her home," I couldn't believe my ears! Doctor said, "I suppose you have other children," and I said, "No, I don't." So, breaking all of the hospital rules, he said that I was to feed her before I brought her home. I was told to put on all of the things they gave me, and to do everything the nurse told me and feed that child! I was really scared to death but tried to be very composed and listened intently to every little thing I was told. This was quite an experience for the nipples on the bottles had to be cut and placed in her mouth a certain way, so she would be able to nurse. Because of her mouth she was unable to suck on the nipple and so by placing the cut nipple up and down she was able to get milk, and you had to hold her up in such a way she did not strangle. Quite an experience, but I made it.

At eighteen months she had the roof of her mouth closed and did very well. Ivan took Kathy and me to St Louis to Children's Hospital and we were there a week to ten days for the surgery. I lost at least ten pounds and was so very glad to get home with Kathy. Down there I was unable to get anything to eat after four o'clock in the afternoon. Due to hospital regulations I couldn't leave and unless I got something like a candy bar there was nothing to eat. While there I was told she would have to have speech therapy, but she didn't. They said I did it, but my thoughts were that I didn't do any more for her than I would do for any other child. She did a good job trying to talk and I was so thrilled when she said, Mom, Mom, Mom. She did well and grew like any other little one would.

Ralph, our neighbor, got really sick and was in the hospital for some time. He had problems with his bowels and seemed to be getting weaker. I know he got so thin I was afraid I might bring him some germs by just visiting him. His mother was insisting we visit. During his stay Wilma had a son named Rick. Dr. Strong was Ralph's doctor, and breaking all of the rules, doctor went to the nursery and got the baby and brought him down to Ralph's room and asked Ralph, "Now look at this boy, isn't he something for you to live for?" Ralph made a turn around after that and got well. What a joy to see someone so sick get well!!

Before building and after, I continued to work on the yard to get it so we could mow, as there were so many rose bushes, flowers and other things in the yard. Out back, there were sheds, a long table and many pieces of trees and some boards stretched over where she worked on vegetables and other things outside but needed to be replaced badly. I was always hoping I wouldn't upset her making the changes that I felt needed to be done.

As the months went by we tore sheds down in the back yard. The bench was not replaced. The fence was taken down around the garden, and that worked really well, and you could easily get into the garden without going through the gate. Ivan thought the chickens would bother the garden, but they didn't. Hurrah!! Everything was looking so much better than before. Flowers were moved to make room for mowing and that was good. We seemed to be busy the year around.

We attended Monroe Christian Church in Monroe City, but our membership was still at Huntington Christian Church. We promised that we would leave our membership there until it closed. Records show we joined the Monroe Christian Church in 1962. I know that we were attending in Monroe City while Rev. Simpson was minister and Rev. Lierle started in July of 1957. Many records have been destroyed. This is unbelievable!

Ivan wanted his mother and Virgil to live with us. I told Ivan, "Now, the ball is in your field and you have to decide what to do, we have to do something!" She cannot stay in the baby bed any longer. We either have to build on to this house, or have a trailer placed out back for Virgil to stay in, or he has to go to town. Ivan finally decided to ask him to go to town and live. I'll never forget that day. He cried like a baby! I felt so sorry for him. I told him he could eat any of his meals here anytime he wanted to and that seemed to ease some of the pain.

If we had only built a place to ourselves this would not have happened! Nevertheless, Virgil found a room in a family home in Monroe City that he could rent, and he moved to town. He seemed fairly content after that and spent his days out here and watched Kathy as she played outside, and I worked in the garden or yard or doing whatever that needed to be done.

Another experience I remember really well was with the guineas. For some reason they liked Ivan but didn't like me. I was to feed them, and they had little ones and so I proceeded to do the feeding and two of older guinea's raised up and started coming for my head, one from the right side and the other from the left. I had a stick in my hand and swung it and hit one in the head and she laid on the ground like she was going to die, and I could have cared less about that. I said, "Go ahead and die, I don't care if you do!" Funny now but I was very serious when it happened. I told Ivan after that, "they are yours and you feed them. I'll feed anything else but the guineas!" Very strange to say the least!

We hired young boys to help Ivan do the farming and kept them pretty busy. When we married, a boy by the name of Jimmy Clark was working for Ivan. A family by the name of Shelton's lived across the road and it seems they didn't live there long and a family by the name of Ogle's moved in. They had six children and Jimmy met one of the girls, by the name of Velda, and really liked her. We would tease him that he had to hurry after work and get across the road. That took a while but very much a couple now.

As the years passed we tried different boys in the neighborhood. Think the Bunn boys were next as I remember the older Bunn boy helping me when we built the house to refinish floors. His brother helped later after Bernie quit and the Gough boys were next, that helped us a lot. Even the Gough girls, Carolyn and Marilyn helped on the yard as all of it was hard to keep up for me. It seemed that my hands were always full to say the least. One year Dennis, Marvin and Lois's son, came to our rescue to help us and we were thrilled, but that didn't work out either as he had so many things he wanted to take off for. With farming that made things very difficult. I did most of the cooking. I made all of my clothes and Ivan's mother's clothes and gave her permanents as that made it less expensive to do that rather than go to the beauty shop. Maud was not a fussy person about her looks. People thought I made her look so much better after being in the family. I enjoyed sewing for Maud and myself. I tried to help her to look better. Sometimes you do things for people you don't think much about it.

The winter time when Ivan would go coon hunting, I would sit up and sew making nearly all of her clothing and mine also. As the girls came along, I sewed for them. Busy, but enjoyable.

The road by this house was a gravel road and the dust in the summer time was terrible. You could clean your house in the morning and by afternoon you could write your name on everything in the house even when you would keep the windows and doors closed. One time we had company to come from California and visit and I cleaned and worked so hard trying to have everything clean, and by the time they came, everything was dusty. They said they were going to Palmyra for a little while, and while they were gone I cleaned again and again everything got covered with dust. There was no stopping the dust it seemed. Years later they black topped the road and my, what a difference!

We were hoping that we would have blacktop to Route A but that didn't happen and to this day it hasn't either. I doubt if it ever happens, but sure wish that it would. I remember when Kathy was going to school she would wait at the road for the bus and the dust was so bad you couldn't see her standing there waiting. This was always a busy road as it is the road going to the Missouri Central Stone and lots of trucks hauling rock.

I remember sometime in the latter fifties, there was a knock on the door and I answered, and it was Dwight Henderson and he asked me to be the organist at the Monroe City Christian Church. I was so surprised and immediately said, "I can't do that!" His answer was, "We think you can, and we would like very much for you to try." I finally said I would try.

He told me that Miss Edna Boulware would help me, as I had not had any organ lessons at all. I met with Miss Edna and she spent about ten to fifteen minutes with me and left and said, "You use the stops as you want to, you will be fine." My thoughts were "What Have I Gotten Myself Into, God Help Me!" I began to work on pieces, and Miss Edna had given me one book of organ music and I practiced using different stops. I think I started in 1957, however the records don't show that, but I remember Rev. Simpson and Dean Lierle.

By the history of the church, one stopped as minister and the other started. I vividly remember Lierle telling me how to play for a wedding and that, "Music must start and never stop until at a given time." He was always very precise on his instructions. One of the times I was playing my left leg shook so much from being scared. I wouldn't dare try to put it down on any pedal. I felt I would hit several not just one and that would be bad for anyone to do. I finally got accustomed to the bench, organ and etc. A lot to remember and every week I would practice at least once a week and sometimes more.

When Kathy was only two, Ivan and I had the misfortune of losing a son, that was probably four to five months old when I had to be taken to the hospital and it was a stillborn birth. We were very sad about this happening, but such is life and things do happen beyond our control. Guess some things are not meant to be and this was the way it was. The baby was buried in the family plot in Monroe City.

After this happened and for a while Ivan had to do the laundry. We bought a Maytag washer and dryer and it was put upstairs near the back door. This was very handy and easy to get to and has been there ever since. The old wringer washer was sold, and tubs were kept for a while, for dressing chickens, and then got rid of them. I was so happy about that as had wanted that soon after we were in the house, of course one of the main reasons was that we needed to save water.

Ivan's brother Bennie and his wife Julia had two children. They were Chris and Doris. I think I have mentioned them before and on October 27, 1963 Chris married Pat Gosney in the Monroe City Christian Church.

The Huntington School closed before Kathy was old enough to go and all children were bussed to Monroe City. I was giving music lessons to different ones in the community and taught probably ten to twelve different ones how to play.

As the years rolled by so many things happened; babies born, deaths of friends and family and, if listed the names would go on and on. Kathy was going to be in school when I was expecting another little girl. In fact, I was in the hospital for 72 days before our second daughter was born. I had gone to the hospital three times and the last time I decided to just stay as with Ivan farming it was so very hard to manage things. A private room at the hospital cost twenty-one dollars a day, insurance paid ten and I paid eleven or vice versa. Not for sure which, but nearly the same and for someone to come here and stay would cost eight dollars an hour, so the hospital seemed the cheapest. That way I would be there without any worry about going. Ivan was there most every day and time went fairly fast. He was the chief cook and looked after Kathy with Virgil's help, and of course, his mother too.

I spent my days looking forward to the mail, watching soap operas on TV and the show *Let's Make a Deal*. Sometimes I would try to guess who would be the next one to go by my door. One day I received a small package in the mail. I couldn't imagine who it was from, and I noticed the return and it was from Norway. How wonderful, for someone to remember me so far away! I knew that Lloyd and Mildred were there and tearing the brown paper off the package I had a metal Sucrets box and inside was a beautiful pair of earrings. I'm sure they are hand painted, sort of leaf design and so very pretty. I still cherish them. They were so very nice to me. Always remembering me with such nice things. Lloyd was in the Army Air Force and stationed in Oslo, Norway for several years.

I also found that Kathy had gained a lot of weight during my stay in the hospital, and she could not wear any of her clothes that I had for her. That was not a good thing, as we had to figure out what she would wear to school. I was not able to go buy clothes for I couldn't leave the hospital, but some way we got that taken care of. I told Ivan not to make so much gravy and have more vegetables and fruit and maybe she would lose some.

A CLOSE CALL AND MORE ABOUT FAMILY

One day when Ivan had gone down into the pasture to check on something, Kathy decided to go see him and started out into the north pasture fairly close to the house. A large sow that had little pigs was in this pasture, and guarding her piglets, she started after Kathy. She was near a pond dam and rolled down the embankment away from the sow and stopped before getting into the water. The sow decided not to bother her and went back to her pigs and Kathy began to cry. She was scared half to death, and Virgil went to see about her and very soon Ivan came also. Kathy had a scar on the back of her head and one of her arms had been in the sow's mouth but was not seriously hurt. Ivan brought her to the doctor and she was checked over and found okay. That very morning the news of the accident had reached the hospital, and everyone knew but me. I sensed something was wrong the way people acted and the minister that always goes around seeing patients asked, "Is everything alright at home?" I thought that is a silly question to ask me, but didn't say anything I just answered, "Yes, I guess they're okay." He later told me that he knew by my answer that I didn't know what had happened.

Between eleven and twelve o'clock in came Ivan with my gown and I asked, "Why are you here this time of day?" He said, "Oh I just brought you your gown." I knew something was wrong and said, "What has happened?"

He finally told me about Kathy and the sow and brought Kathy to the hospital to have her checked out and she had spent the night on first floor and I was on third. I said, "Are you sure she has all of her fingers, and okay in every way?" He said, "Yes."

I was so thankful that Kathy was okay, and with a little help from others we got her ready for school. She was very thankful when I got home and so was I.

Judy was born September 25, 1964 and was fine, but only five pounds and half an ounce. Don't think I could have a big baby if I wanted to. Judy did fine, and in few days I was able to bring her home.

I never told that in my stay at the hospital I met up with a gal from near Center, and we became best of friends. She had gall bladder problems as well as pregnant and was in and out of the hospital and we would even knock on the wall to see if the other one knocked back, so as to know the other was there. She passed away in the last few years, and it is hard to believe she is gone. She was several years younger than me. This happened several times during my stay, she had gall-bladder problems. Many times in life we find it isn't just you, that has problems in life.

Kids grew, time passed, and the busy life on the Lehenbauer farm was busier than ever. Ivan's mother was quite a challenge at times. I remember nearly every fall, Ivan wanted to go to Colorado deer hunting with Lloyd. He and Mildred were always after us to come and we did go a number of years. We also noticed that every time we were to go somewhere Ivan's mother would either get sick or she would fall, and then our trip was postponed or something. Then we started not telling her we were going until we had to. That wasn't easy to do either.

I remember taking Lloyd and Mildred a case of eggs, either 15 or more, sometimes up to 30 dozen, which is a lot of eggs. They would be so thrilled to get them and two or three months later we would get the phone call that their fresh eggs were now gone. How they wished they had more. Ha! They were serious, but funny to me. They didn't care if they had had them a month or so they thought they were fresher than those bought in the store, and I am sure they were.

The house needed painting and I took on the job, and what a challenge! In order to have peace of mind I would take both girls outside. Would carry the baby pen outside also and put Judy in that and make sure Kathy was okay with whatever she was playing with and then get up on the ladder and paint. It was quite a task, but I did make it. Once in a while I had help like maybe Lois for a while and sometimes, I just stayed with it and little by little it was accomplished.

We got word that Doris Kraus, Bennie Lehenbauer's daughter, had a son named Curtis born in Kansas City, KS in January, of 1960.

Lloyd's mother Alma had her first stroke in July in 1966 and recovered some but not real great. Then in October of the same year she had the second stroke and was taken to a home in Hannibal. Both of their girls, Dorothy and Mary Sue were there for a while, but she just wasn't coming out of this. I saw her several times and she would yawn so naturally but never did wake up to talk or act like she knew anyone was near. She died a few weeks later. We were very careful what we said, as you never know what they hear and what they don't. She finally passed away in October 1966.

Such a sad time but she just seemed to not be able to get well. Uncle Baxter was very lost without her and was almost helpless in the kitchen. I checked on him every once in a while. Found he was eating oatmeal three times a day and so I tried to help a little but that was very hard also. Uncle Baxter finally moved to Monroe City and was neighbors to his brother David Watts and the two of them had a lady hired to cook and look after both of them. This lasted for a few years.

Ivan's mother got really weary on her legs and for years walked inside a metal frame loaned to us by the Health Department in New London. Once in a while she would turn that over also but most of the time, she was able to stay upright. Then later, she was sick and not herself. She was confused and was not sleeping nights. After a few weeks of this we decided we had to put her in the nursing home in Palmyra, MO. and did. She was there a number of months and I remember one Christmas we decided to bring her home here for the day and I was frankly scared she might be a problem when it was time for her to go back. Instead by three o'clock, she said she needed to get back so she could be sure to have her evening meal and I was so surprised and so she kept insisting and we finally took her back before we had dinner that evening. I was so very surprised at her request. Bennie and Julia were here that day also. A day we all enjoyed but had a surprising ending. You never know what is going on in someone else's mind.

Ivan's mother passed away February 28, 1968 at 85 years old. The next day after her death Chris and Pat had their first child a little girl born February 29, 1968.

I found out years later that my sister Jean secretly married Junior Beedle November 13, 1969. Brad and Jean and Junior and his wife occasionally double dated and later switched husbands and wives. Sounds confusing but they did it.

Virgil got sick and was sent to Columbia to the University Hospital and died on July 8, 1970 at the age of 61. That was a shock! We were told he was doing fine and suddenly; he was dead. Ivan and Bennie asked the hospital for papers about his death and the papers really didn't show any particular thing as to the cause of death. Virgil had typhoid fever when in his latter teens, and that went into rheumatoid arthritis. This he suffered with the rest of his life. His knees were bent, and hands bent at the wrist. He would have been over six feet tall if he could stand erect. He was unable to keep a job in the condition he was in, at least that is what he thought; Ivan and I often wondered but didn't talk about it, we just let it go.

As I struggle to write this so many things were happening, and it is impossible to remember everything; just bits and pieces of things. I have my Farmer's Elevator calendars of the events and that helps me a lot with dates and also helps me to get things in the right sequence. I only have them starting in 1974 and so the previous part I remembered. Funny what you can remember, and now in my eighties I seem to forget quite a bit. I always thank God for what I can remember and what I can do, and for each day I have on this earth.

I felt very close to my uncles that lived fairly close. Both Uncles, David and Baxter, had children but they didn't live close; so, I tried to do what I could to help them out. Uncle David lived north of Monroe City and the boys moved him to Monroe City, so he could have more help. Uncle Baxter, after several months, finally moved to Monroe also, next door to David. That was unusual but very nice. They finally hired a lady that took care of both men and saw to some of the cooking and needs they had, and that was certainly nice for them.

As time went on Uncle Baxter was put in the nursing home in Pittsfield, IL. Mary Sue had gone to Quincy School of Nursing and she was acquainted with Illinois. She met her future husband, Gordon Batley, who was from Pittsfield during her time studying to be a nurse at Quincy. Ill. Mary Sue was acquainted with the place and I think she and her husband were living in Chicago, IL. He was there several months and one time I took dad to see him. Dad was very silent that day and later told me, "He didn't want to ever be put in a place like that." I really feel that is the reason for his death on the pond dam, but of course you never know.

I found out by phone that Uncle Baxter was not expected to live and so I went over there to be with him. So happy to help out the family as none of them could be with him. He died September 30, 1971, and I was with him when it happened.

I know that Ivan's father died in 1945 on my birthday and Ivan had to run the farm and took care of his mother and brother. He did not join the service for those reasons. Ivan said he was a disappointment all the way around and I asked, "Why do you say that?" He said, "I came after Christmas, and I wasn't a girl." He was a very nice and caring man, that is for sure. I was very proud to have him as a husband. His birthday was December 28th.

We talked of buying more land, but didn't as we didn't have any boys coming on and it was hard to find help on the farm. We could have bought land on both sides of us but talking it over we knew we couldn't handle any more. We also knew that we were both getting ourselves stretched so far, we couldn't do anymore. We struggled to find someone to work in the hay when we were baling and needing help to put the bales in the barn.

Chris and Pat had their second child born August 2, 1971, a son.

We finally bought a *Harvestore* to help store the hay and grain. That was definitely good for having feed for the calves to eat so they would fatten for selling. I worked putting a garden two places; one in the garden here at the house and behind the barn was another garden. I spent many days running the tractor in the field. We had an old M Farmall, and I drove that for years. I always said, "If you were ten pounds too heavy a few days on that tractor and it beat it off your rear." Ha!

On January 6, 1972 I received a call from mother saying, "Come Quick, I think your dad is dead!" I ran out to tell Ivan and we went down there right away but the house was open and no one there. I couldn't understand where everyone was. I looked and looked and no sign of anyone around. I didn't know what to do! I even called Wilson's Funeral Home, but they said they had not had enough time to go anywhere. So, finally, after several more minutes someone was coming from over the hill, across the road on the Herron Place and it was the Floyd's; Jim and Edna, Wilson's and mother. It was all over; dad was dead! Quite a shock, but that was that. I heard later, in a few days, that dad had told Shuck's that doctor had given him some digitalis pills to take for his heart. He had not said anything to mother or me so who knows; he may have never taken any, not sure. I turned in and called my sister who lived in Vandalia, about 30 miles away. I called several other friends and family members.

Arrangements were made for the visitation and funeral. Looking over the crowd at the church who should I see, but Lloyd and Dale Watts, who had made the trip from Colorado. That meant so very much. That always showed how special, and how close we were as family. I couldn't help but think of what dad had said when he was at Pittsfield, IL. Such is life! Mother said he ate breakfast and then went out to chop ice for the cattle and died. A doctor told me afterward that many times after a person has eaten a warm breakfast, and then go outside in the cold and suck in the cold air in their lungs that that kills them, especially if their heart is weak. This all left a big hole to fill without Dad.

It was quite a celebration of life through the Wilson Funeral Home, Ariel Church and burial in Monroe City. The people that showed, it was one to remember. Mother continued to live on the home place and seemed happy there. As happy as you can be after losing your mate of fifty-two years with all of their years spent at the Watts Homestead. I tried to look after mother and saw to her needs of things that were hard for her to accomplish; such as the yard, garden and etc. So many days to mow her lawn and mine took eight hours to do it and I had to take my lawn mower down there to get that done. Quite a challenge for sure. We finally gave up on the garden as I said I could give her all she wanted to eat rather than have a garden.

In the next few months ahead, we decided that we must have a sale of implements and things that mother no longer needed. So, we were able to get that done. The sale was in April of that year. I encouraged mother to get rid of things she didn't need and while hard, she did well considering everything.

One of the implements that Dad had was a John Deere tractor and he always started it with a pull on the flywheel. Ivan, my husband, told him there is a starter on the tractor, why don't you use the starter? Dad would shrug his shoulders and never did try and Ivan after talking to him, dad still wouldn't try to use it. He thought it wouldn't work. So, the day of the sale Ivan had cleaned all of the dirt, grease, nails and etc. from around the starter and was able to get the tractor running by using the starter. To think that my dad wasted so much energy, pulling on the flywheel.

I finally said, "Can't we buy a riding mower down here and mother did, and that was wonderful!" I also bought her a push lawn mower from TG&Y and that mower is still running. I hired a boy to help me mow and in fact to do the mowing and he kept taking parts off the mower. I said something about it to mother and she was very unhappy and so I stopped him from mowing. Sure didn't need someone taking parts off such as shield's and etc. What you deal with when you try to get someone to help you.

Mother kept having heart palpitation spells. She had had them for years. I had slept with her several nights after dad's passing thinking I might lose both parents, but thank God, I didn't. The medication she had taken for years when she would have a spell caused her to have diarrhea, which was not a good thing, so I talked her into going to a different doctor and she did. He wanted her to go on some heart medication, and after she did she never had another spell after that, which was wonderful.

I was still giving music lessons, and of course had the two girls to look after. I helped mother whenever she had card parties, CWF and anything else that she had to do extra work to have in her home. That was quite a challenge also. I was in hopes Jean would help, but she thought she was too far away and couldn't do that.

Many challenges it seemed to keep up with the girls at school, organist at church and later started playing for both Wilson Funeral Home and Garner Funeral Home. Some way, with all of the family appointments, and mother's, as well as the things going on the farm and farm animals, I was busy from morning to night.

Starting the year 1974, the girls were both sick with sore throats and etc in January. We finally took Judy to St Louis to see a doctor about allergies. We found that some of her allergies were food related. Chocolate and eggs were some of her allergies. Had Kathy tested also and found cheese, cabbage and anything that went through the molding process she was allergic to. Of course, dog and cat dander were also in there and it was clean, clean, and clean some more. Anything with dampness affected them both and Ivan also. They were better after a while and knowing what foods to not have. Many times, when Judy would cough at night, I would ask her if she had chocolate today, and she would generally say, "Yes." That wasn't easy to say the least. When Judy was riding the bus very often children wanted the windows open and the dust and dampness came in the window and she would come home so stopped up she couldn't breathe.

Chris and Pat had their third child August 2, 1974, another boy.

Kathy had a great group of friends that were her classmates and several times a year she would have a bunking party and invite girls here. They really enjoyed their visit and now have many stories to tell of happenings here and what I had for them to eat. I enjoyed them so much also, never a dull moment. Kathy also enjoyed playing in the band and the special times they would perform. She graduated from high school in May of 1975. Her plans were to go to college somewhere. She later decided to go to Kirksville to school.

Friends and neighbors died, and life was one busy time. Ivan was also enjoying night hunts for coons. I was on the committee preparing for a soup supper for the band, also I took a big part in CWF and on Wednesday nights I had choir to practice with.

My Uncle David Watts, another one of dad's brothers come up with cancer of the breast in April of 1974 and had surgery in Hannibal in April to fix him so you could be with him at the last. Doctors said if they hadn't done the surgery that the smell would be so strong you couldn't stay in the room with him. So, they did surgery and I never did notice any odor while visiting him at Paris, MO in the nursing home. At that time there wasn't one in Monroe City.

One of the ladies of our club Mrs. Joe (LuElsie) Johnson lived at the end of the blacktop south of here where they used to call Sidney. They had six or seven children and one of their girls, named Helen, married a Cornelius. She had a beautiful voice. In fact, several of them sang together and Helen slipped away and made a name for herself. One time in 1975 she sang at a cancer benefit in Ralls County. The family attended Ariel Church and sang at a lot of functions around the area. Helen finally went to Nashville, TN where she did a lot of singing engagements.

During that year Uncle Leo's sister Lora Hager died and was buried at Monroe City. President Nixon resigned in August of that year. It seemed there was always something happening. A lot of turmoil in the leadership of the United States.

The girls had lots of problems with allergies. Kathy had to have braces again on her teeth. She had worn them years ago but had to start again, but she always did it and didn't complain. I was also helping mother with her doctor's appointments.

Uncle David was still in Paris at the nursing home and he gradually got worse and died June 17, 1975. I saw him several times in Paris as I always felt sorry for him as one son lived in Arizona and the other one in Moline, IL. A good distance for them to travel, especially Daniel who lived in Sun City, AZ. Knowing that for a man to have breast cancer is very unusual and so I knew by this that it was very prevalent in the Watts family. Several others had cancer later. I also wondered about Grandmother Watts as it was told she died of ulcers of the stomach, but, maybe she had cancer and back then they didn't know.

Elmer Colliver, neighbor across from Uncle Baxter's, died on September 12, 1975. His wife continued to live there. The way I remember Elmer died quickly, they didn't have any children.

Several years ago, we helped the Rothfuss family to move from an "Old House" out on the highway to a place just east of here. They had been renting for years and had never had electricity or water in her home. Talk about being thrilled; she was that indeed. I felt so happy for her as she couldn't have been happier.

Ivan began having trouble with his arms and legs and he felt he was losing use of them, so he decided to go to Rochester, Minnesota to the Mayo Clinic. He did not want to be like his brother Virgil and have trouble getting around, so we decided to just go and wait until they could see us. We were told that is the only way to do it so that is what we did. I took the sewing machine, crockpot, and probably reading material as we had no idea how long we would be there. We rented a basement apartment and walked to the clinic. You would think there weren't many people around until you would get inside and "My Goodness, what a crowd!" I think we were there at least a week and half before we got to see anyone. I remember they called us up to the desk and asked if we would go home and come back later and we said, "No!" We didn't have time to come back and hoped to get in very soon. We sat for another fifteen or twenty minutes and were called and were told, "Be here in the morning at eight o'clock." We said, "Okay" and left. The next morning, we were there on time and tests started. Their procedure taking care of a large group of people was quite something. I'll have to say they knew how to manage a group of people, and when we entered the building people were coming in on all sides of the building. It was unbelievable. Different tests were run with blood and urine and they would have a way of marking them and you put them in large containers in the hall.

We met up with a couple from Chicago that was very nice, and we kept running into them. After introducing ourselves we met many times of evenings having dinner together which was nice as always. The gentleman said whatever is wrong with you is wrong with me as we have the same symptoms. As time went on, we learned that the man had cancer, which was rather shocking, and Ivan had arthritis. They said his hands looked like rheumatoid, but it was mainly osteoarthritis. Their main prescription was aspirin to relieve pain and not much else. We continued to be in contact with the Chicago people and learned that the gentleman's health went from bad to worse and he died in February of 1976. How tragic, we were so sorry to hear.

LOT'S GOING ON AND A WEDDING IN COLORADO AND SOME SUDDEN DEATHS

The year 1976 was started off with Marvin and Lois having the New Year's party of which we usually took turns. Kathy left for Kirksville to go to college, we attended a funeral at Wilson's Funeral home and a rehearsal supper and wedding at the end of the week. This was Henry and Margaret McClintock's daughter, Lee Ann. Every week was filled with club, choir music and doctor's appointments. Judy was busy in junior high and she loved sports. We had quite a bit of snow this winter and this time we had six inches. We always made time for our girls and the things they wanted to do especially when they were in school.

Aunt Angelea Watts married Albert Bixler and she was the next to die, March 31, 1976. She had cancer also. This was the one that I spoke about. Albert was Maud's (Ivan's mother's), brother. The deaths seemed endless, one after another. They had one daughter, Juanita, who lived in Columbia, MO. Albert went up there to be with her rather than be alone. Seemed funny for Ivan and me to have the same Aunt and Uncle when we married. Aunt Angelea's funeral was April 1, 1976 at the Monroe City Christian Church.

Our friend and neighbor, Sterling Carter, felt he also had the same symptoms and probably the same health issue. He also had cancer. How sorry we were to hear but felt so very thankful that two people with the same symptoms as Ivan's and they both had cancer and Ivan didn't. We were so very thankful and yet no matter who you talk to, you never know when it is your time and what you might have. One of the many things you learn in life. Sterling died in June of 1976.

The rest of the year we came home and did the harvesting and things we needed to do on the farm to finish up another crop season, taking care of animals and etc. Lots of things to do for winter.

Aunt Angelea was taken to the hospital in Hannibal on February 13 and came home the twentieth and then entered again; and Aunt Lera also. They were both in intensive care and both had cancer. I was so sorry to hear that. Aunt Angelea died March 31, 1976.

Friends were dying also, and a special cousin. One of Ivan's mother's favorite cousin's died in Illinois. Track meets were also starting up and Judy was a very busy gal, as well as the rest of us.

Both of the girls had allergies and I finally took them to St. Louis to a doctor down there to see what they were allergic to. Kathy was allergic to cheese and anything that goes through the molding process. Doctor told me that you didn't have to worry about Velvetta. My answer was, "That is the only cheese I use." I knew that was not right, as she was so stopped up she could hardly get her breath when I had cheese sandwiches one evening, as Ivan was gone, and I didn't have any meat cooked. We came in from outside and had been working in the garden and fixed something easy and quick. Judy was allergic to chocolate and eggs as well as dust and mold. Wasn't that wonderful! Needed something else to do besides clean and all of the rest.

Looks like by the calendar that the winter was mighty cold. Several funerals and the usual meetings, music and family and friends visiting, appointments and etc. Mother and Aunt Lillian were still hanging in there. Girls were very busy. One in high school, and the other in college. I was still helping mother and Aunt Lillian.

It was November of 1976 when the news came to us that Joe Chisham had died the night before. Joe was one of the older Chisham boys that used to ride in the old truck bringing us ice.

The year 1977 Helen Johnson Cornelius was in the Quincy area and popping up here and there. Her parents lived just south of me at the end of the blacktop. She was a good singer and made headlines in the news of her being asked to appear different places.

It was in May when the phone rang, and who should call but Lloyd wanting us to come to Dale and Patsy's wedding. I said, "We couldn't do that because of crop season and strawberries." Lloyd replied, "There are airplanes!" He wanted me to come without Ivan. My thoughts were, I have never ridden on an airplane, to go by myself, it was hard to think positive about that. I finally decided to go by myself and Lois would take me to Quincy to the airport. Hoping I had everything taken care of, at least that would hold until I got back. When I got on the plane it was so much smaller than I thought it would be, but everything was okay, but so different. My, but that plane was noisy, and I couldn't help but be a little scared. I asked a young man, in fact I think we were the only ones on the plane, if he minded me talking to him and he said, "No!" That made me happy, and I felt so much better! The young man said he had made the trip many times.

Lloyd and Mildred lived in Colorado Springs and they were there to pick me up when the plane landed. It was an enjoyable trip! When my stay was over I came back to St. Louis and then took the small plane to Quincy the way I did going there. When I got to Quincy there was hardly anyone around and so I chose a seat and began to wait as I didn't see Ivan anywhere around. I waited and waited and thought, "My Dear Husband has forgotten me." I waited over an hour and then he finally showed. Was I glad!! I had to just sit and wait hoping he would remember.

Came home to the busy schedule of swim lessons for Judy, piano lessons, club meetings and etc. I was still giving music lessons and was the organist at church. I had had someone to fill in for me while I was gone that one Sunday. I think it was Ronnie Mayes. He probably played the piano as no one would play the organ. How did I get so lucky?

Every year Ivan fed out some young cattle and they were sold in the spring. We had hogs also, as well as chickens. So, you never run out of something to do, that was for sure. Not for sure who our hired hand was at this time but if we didn't have one Ivan would call on me. I was always glad to help him out and some way I was able to get the cooking done also so that was good as you always have to eat it seems.

I remember being called over to Bill and Nora Lee's house and Bill was very sick. I went there, and Nora Lee was saying that Bill was having problems with his heart. I said, "Don't change his clothes that might be too much," but I think that did happen and I decided to drive them to the hospital rather than call and wait on the ambulance. Bill told me over and over that he was going to die, and I told him, "No, you aren't!" I drove as fast as I dared to the hospital. I had the air blowing on him and away we went. We made it and I was so thankful about that, and it was his heart and with God's help we made it.

On Sunday, September 11, 1977, who should drive in but Bill and Peg Hulse and mother. This was Jean's oldest son and wife. They had stopped and picked up mother on their way here. We had a wonderful visit! While they were here they went to the garden and picked cherry tomatoes and the yellow pear-shaped ones. I was glad to share them, and Peggy was eating them one right after another. I said, "Don't eat those tomatoes, they aren't clean!" She replied, "Oh Aunt

Wanda, you have to eat over a peck of dirt before you die!" We had a chuckle over that, and she went on eating. That night the phone rang at 1:30 or 2:00 a.m. I answered, and it was Jean, my sister, saying that Bill and Peg had been in a car accident near Kansas City. Peggy was dead, and Bill not expected to live; he was critical. I was floored! How could this be? I remembered what was said that afternoon, and thought you never know what is going to happen or when. I was saying before they left, "Be very careful!" And Bill gave me a big hug and said, "Don't worry, we'll be just fine."

A few days went by and Bill had not died. The family decided to go ahead and have the visitation for Peggy on Wednesday, September 14th and the funeral the next day in Farber at the Presbyterian Church. They said that when they lowered her in the ground that Bill died. That was the end of a wonderful couple! Bill always said after dad died, "Aunt Wanda, don't worry about grandmother. I will help you take care of her." Now he is gone? I couldn't believe it! The day of Peg's funeral was the day we got word that Bill died. His funeral was on Saturday the 17th at the same church, just three days later.

In 1978 the year started the same except it was at Lois and Marvin's. It was basketball games for Judy, music lessons, piano lessons for me and several deaths. Mother seemed to need more help and every week friends die, choir continues and hard to fit everything in a busy schedule. Kathy was here and working at Dr. Avilla's office. She had finished her two years at Kirksville taking business classes. She was real happy she was able to get the job for a husband and wife team.

We would see that mother had groceries even in the dead of winter. Sometimes we had lots of snow; nine and a half inches and 10 degrees below zero. Gee! That's cold! Things didn't seem to let up. If it wasn't one thing it was another. Ivan and I also took groceries to Bill and Nora Lee Lehenbauer as it was too slick for them to get out and we had a truck with a four-wheel drive.

Sometime prior to July 1st of this year, one gentleman, Bill Lehenbauer, who was only a cousin, but seemed like an Uncle, died. That was one of many funerals I played for; this time it was at Garner's. So many people were dying it seemed. It was noon when the phone rang, and it was Lizzie Rothfuss saying, "Come quick!" Something was wrong with Gene, her son. Jeff Ogle, a neighbor boy, was working for us and we immediately got up from the table and left in the car for the Rothfuss house, which was a short distance from here. Gene was very sick and the first thing the guys had to do was help him to the bathroom. He collapsed when he came from there and he begged not to go to the hospital, but we did call an ambulance. They were unable to revive him, and I was so sorry to see him die. This was the family that had lived for years in an old house on south side of highway 36 that didn't have electricity and no modern convenience to speak of. Her husband had died, and she was living there with two boys and the other boy was in Arizona. Mrs. Lizzie Rothfuss and Gene had decided to buy a house just east of me and she was so thrilled. I will never forget how she talked about having lights with a flip of the switch and she was so very happy. It made me feel so good to see someone that happy. You don't realize how little it takes to make people happy until you see this before your eyes. It was such a pleasure to help her move.

In 1979, one of the big things for Judy was the track meet in Centralia. At their track meet the Monroe City boys won first place by seven points, and the girls won first by four points. Not too bad for the school. Judy ran in something but don't remember exactly what race; my notes don't tell me that.

Later in the summer, Judy detasseled corn in fields with a group of others and was paid for doing it. She was excited about doing that but found it really was not easy and an eye opener to say the least. I think this was her first time working for someone else. The pay was not the greatest for all of the work they did.

I didn't have very many weddings this year, but thirteen funerals. Lots of music lessons, both Judy's and ones I gave. Appointments, birthdays, church and family get togethers. July 14th we even had company from Connecticut. This was Marjorie Bixler and her son Donald and wife Ginny. Marjorie was a niece of Ivan's mother. This was the first time they had been here, and we were certainly glad to have them. We always corresponded but neither one got to visit either place after that.

Lloyd and Mildred got to come in July also; a nice short visit. Lloyd always made time to see me whenever possible. Steve and Dorothy (Lloyd's sister), and Aunt Margaret (Alma's sister) came to visit us also. That was so very nice.

Hedy Rothfuss and Tom Wubberhorst got married at West Ely and Reva and Earl Rothfuss's daughter and their son, Levering, were on the Johnny Carson Show this fall. He was quite a musician and Hedy does quite well also. Reva and I went to school together and she married a neighbor and friend of Ivan's, Earl Rothfuss. A son of the lady I had just told about moving to a place east of me. Even though we are not in, shall I say, 'A Special Place', we have several that have done quite well that lived in the area. Not all areas can say that.

While we are talking about celebrities, Helen Johnson Cornelius was raised just south of me and she did quite well with her music. She is in her 70's now but has done a lot of singing with different ones in Nashville. She and her sister Judy sang together also. Helen and her sister and the O'Neal girls did quite a bit of singing and I accompanied them several times.

The rest of the year was very busy. Ivan loved to hunt and was always trading dogs, going to dog hunts of a night and water racing in the daytime. Not too often but sometimes on weekends. I had a few weddings; one for a cousin at Big Creek Church east of here. You never know when you might be asked. Lots of church work, CWF, Sunday School, Church and etc. Judy was busy with all kinds of sports and youth camp for those going to the Christian Church. Judy also played in the band, just as Kathy did when she was in high school.

Played for a funeral at Big Creek Church for Virgil LaRue. His wife was my teacher in third and fourth grade. We were always very close with them and I was glad to help them out. Playing for someone was always hard to turn down as it was something I could do without too much effort and I seemed to get asked quite a lot. I never liked charging people for something I could do to help them out; whether it was fixing food, taking them to the doctor or whatever. I seemed to always gain from that with only a 'Thank You'. I loved helping others and was given the chance real often.

SURELY NOT A FIRE! AND MORE

I remember July 9, 1980, I was helping Ivan fill the combine with fuel and Ivan was greasing the machine. I had just gathered eggs from the hen house, as the chickens seemed to break the eggs if I didn't. I glanced around, and everything looked fine. The next moment, here came Judy running and said, "Mom, a truck driver said the barn is on fire!" I couldn't believe my ears and got down and looked at the barn and fire was coming from both gable ends. I ran for the house and started praying to save everything.

We thought the fire truck would never get here. Neighbors were gathering, and I felt helpless. Ivan tried to move the machinery from near the barn, but he felt the hair on his arms getting too warm, so he had to quit. They had been hauling square bales of hay and unloading them on the elevator taking them into the barn. A tractor and elevator were still in place. Judy looked for her pony but couldn't find him and we weren't sure where he was. She walked the pasture, but he was not there.

They finally got the fire under control, but the barn was a complete loss. Later the pony was found in the barn, in a corner in the back area. He could have gotten out, but many times an animal will not try when there is a fire. Judy had a cry for a short time but knew it was something you had to accept. That evening the fire truck had to be called back so as to keep it from starting up again as night came on us.

We lost a lot of hay and some harnesses but were very thankful it didn't take anything else at that time. We found that the granary building was so hot you couldn't put your hand on the building and all of our soy beans were in there that had been sold but not yet moved. The hog building south of the barn, we found the rafters were burnt but just didn't burn. We had a 500-gallon tank full of propane near the bins, which were south of the hog barn. We had so much to be thankful for. I prayed and prayed that it wouldn't burn anything else and it didn't! If the other buildings started burning it would have burnt all of them, including the house and maybe would have jumped the road and got the neighbor across the road. What a blessing it didn't!

A week or so later I received a letter from a guy that was going from Washington, Illinois with a picture of the barn burning. He said he and his son were on the highway and decided to come down the lane and take a few pictures of the barn and wrote a nice note. I have them now in my scrapbook and think what a nice gesture that was! Many times, you find others care also, something I will never forget. We have so much to be thankful for and so blessed it wasn't any worse. Later we had a Morton building put in the barn's place.

Looks like in August we got a large piece of cement poured for a patio and basketball court. That made the girls very happy. That was a joy for the girls and visitors when they came.

We had another neighbor pass away, Mrs. Paul Evans. Also, Dr. Prince, who was formerly in charge of Hannibal-LaGrange College died. Always someone dying and so many things going on. Junior Benson who helped run the Hassard Elevator near here was another death that year.

Dorothy and Steve Seward came for visits several times a year and it was always so nice to have them. Mary Sue and Gordon Batley also visited several times a year when they were able to make the trip and that was always nice also.

Ivan got a deer, a large doe, the afternoon of November 15th.

Early in December of 1980, on a Sunday, Mother was cooking breakfast and lightening hit the transformer; and having the electric stove on she saw a large ball of fire and loud pop, and after that mother was very deaf. I got a call from the Colliver's saying mother was there and she was very deaf. I remember going down there and brought her here. I had to play for church that day also but it all got taken care of even though many times you wonder how you are going to manage you simply do with God's help. I brought her out here until we could get the wiring taken care of and knew everything was safe for her at home. She had to have hearing aides after that which really changed her life.

My Aunt Ella Greathouse died on December 10, 1980. That was another one of dad's sisters. The funeral was at Garner Funeral Home on December 12th. Several others died also, there seemed to be no end. If I mentioned all of them there would be no end, for life and death seem to happen every year.

I met the family by the name of Hill. He and one of his sons did plastering for people and I know they did the work here when we built the house. One of the girls married a Lehenbauer; a second cousin of Ivan's and another married an Ogle and is now across the road from me. The father played the violin and wanted me to come and accompany him with the piano. We had many sessions and one time he made the remark, "I don't know what you have, but whatever it is, I have the same thing!" We were able to play instruments together and both of us really enjoyed doing it. He used to want me to come and play at the Nutrition Center and I would say, "I'm not a senior citizen." He did that several years before I finally considered myself a 'Senior Citizen'.

Now in the year of 1981 we were friends with the Elsners and had known them for years and their son, who lived not far from here, took his life. That is really hard to hear about. My Aunt Alma Watts's sister Zora Lynch died on June 17, 1981. She was one of the ladies I saw a few times while growing up.

Judy was chosen as a Junior attendant for the Junior-Senior Banquet the last of April.

April 30, 1981 was the year that President Reagan was shot, as well as three others. Always someone trying to change things by doing bad things.

July 12 was a Sunday and Aunt Lillian had to be put in Levering Hospital after having a slight stroke about noon. She came back to her home in a few days and I hired people to stay with her.

On August 19 I took Aunt Lillian to the clinic in Hannibal and she was sent to the hospital with a compression fracture of the back. She was in the hospital for quite some time and on September 10 I moved Aunt Lillian and Aunt Lera to Monroe Manor in Paris, Missouri. While Aunt Lillian was in the Hannibal hospital they moved her without letting anyone know and they mixed up her dentures with someone else's and as a result she kept complaining that her dentures didn't fit. I finally took her to a dentist in Paris and he said after trying them in her mouth, "They're not her dentures, there is no way that she could wear them." I had never heard of such a thing, but I had to go to the hospital and let them straighten that out. Of course, they couldn't come up with the right dentures, so I told them they should be the ones that pay for her some new ones as it was their fault that they got lost. They did just that, so I made several trips to the dentist in Paris for her new dentures. It was October before she got them. She seemed so much more comfortable with the new ones, so I was relieved.

That year Aunt Lera had her 99th birthday and Uncle Albert had his 95th. Gee, how time was rolling along. They were getting so old and they needed help.

Jim Moyer's died, and the funeral was at Ariel. Joan Glascock and I sang at the funeral. Jim was one of those that played cards and was always taking part in things. One by one people all around me were dying.

On September 21, 1981 Bennie Lehenbauer died. That was Ivan's brother who had a heart attack. That funeral was the week of the 24th. Julia, his wife, was so lost without him.

Now it was fall and Ivan wanted me to get on the tractor and work ground for wheat to be sowed. I was his handy man when he couldn't find anyone else. Lots of things going on. Dorothy and Steve Seward made a short visit. Dorothy is Uncle Baxter's daughter who lives in Kansas City, MO. I was still dealing with CWF, music lessons and of course music for church and trying to see if the girls needed any special things.

Judy was selected as a candidate for Football Queen and she won. That was exciting to know and see. She was crowned at half time on October 9, 1981 and Jeff Spalding was crowned King.

On Friday, October 16 I was practicing at the church for Sunday service when suddenly the door opened and in came a gal saying, "I'm getting married tonight." And she needed me to play for her wedding. I said, "Sorry, I have other plans." She said she couldn't find anyone else to do it. She had already asked Ronnie Mayes and he couldn't do it, so she said she needed me. Later I asked Ronnie and he said, "She never asked me!" I ended up playing for her that evening and canceled my plans to go to a ball game with my family. I felt bad not to go with my family.

I came home, changed clothes and went back with music for the wedding. Can you believe that I was not invited to the reception? And, I was never given a thank you; either personally or by a card. I felt like I had been used. The least she could have done was say thank you. I learned a lesson that night. That no matter who asks I will say no, and not do it unless asked beforehand. Or, shall I say a crisis in some way, for someone I know. I don't go with the church. I just try to do my Christian duty. I do not take a salary to be the church organist; it is a joy to serve the Lord and others.

Aunt Lera was having quite a time as she fell and broke her hip on November 1, and then they found she had pneumonia and they couldn't set the hip until she was over that. Gee! By my notes she died on November 13th with Leukemia and kidney failure. That was hard on Lillian to hear that news. Found out this past week while writing this that Lera had eleven children, the same as her mother. I thought there were only ten. Her last son, Wallace, died and the obituary told of eleven children and no one had ever said anything about her loss and I was told the day of the funeral that she lost a little girl by the name of Marietta. There is always something to learn if you listen or read. Aunt Lera was such a nice, happy person and took care of her family in such a nice way. I always said that hard work and kids didn't kill you, it is everything else.

I have another story to tell about Lera and another member of the family. One morning Aunt Lera was making up biscuits and she didn't have any soda and asked one of her boys to go to the store in Oakwood, which was near them and get some soda. When the boy got to the store he said he needed some soda. The clerk asked, "Do you want wet or dry?" His answer was, as he shrugged his shoulders, "I guess I'll take wet." When he got home from the store his mother said, "I can't make biscuits with that!" This was a joke on the little guy that didn't know the difference.

It seems time keeps marching right along and I went from one year to another doing mostly the same thing with a few things added. I was still seeing after mother and Aunt Lillian; Judy and Kathy both going to school, and with music lessons, organist and handy man, it kept me busy all of the time. I had a lady staying with Aunt Lillian as it was too hard without some help. I kept her in groceries and did her hair quite a bit of the time. She had natural curly hair and it was fairly easy to take care of.

Every year there seemed to be lots of funerals and weddings. Some were people that came to our church and others were people from other churches, but this was norm for the years and time. Many times, I played for funerals at both Wilson's and Garner's funeral homes.

JUDY GRADUATES FROM HIGH SCHOOL AND MORE HAPPENINGS

The year 1982 started off with basketball games. The Monroe City basketball team played the championship game at Mizzou and won the title of second in the state of Missouri. Our friends, Ralph and Wilma Adams went with us to Columbia for the games. That was lots of fun. This was also the year that Judy graduated from high school.

This year there were lots of weddings and deaths it seemed. Reva and Lucille McClintock's brother Nelson, who went to school at Linwood and was in eighth grade when I was in first. Gordon Hill, the father of those in the Hill family, who played the violin while I played the piano and that was so much fun, died suddenly.

He said, "I don't know what you have but whatever it is I have the same thing." We were both able to play whatever piece we had heard and in different keys. That brought quite a chuckle to both of us. I think that many wondered just how we did it. Let us say it is 'God's Gift'.

This was the year that Denise Pfanner and Mark Saunders were married in the Holy Rosary Catholic Church. Also, the year of Donna Berlin and Dennis Long's wedding. The last couple were married in the Holy Rosary Catholic Church, and I was asked to play for the wedding. That was nice, and I enjoyed doing it. I had known the Berlin family for years and that was Donna's request. Everything seemed to work out fine without any problems. I did have one lady say, "I don't know why you were asked to play for the wedding, you're not Catholic!" I said, "I will do whatever they tell me to do and whenever in the service as I am asked to do it." The lady had no comment after that.

There were several more deaths. Rick Mayes drown and the day after his funeral Rick's wife had a baby boy. God always has a plan it seems. What a blessing!

In September we started filling the silo and there were two more deaths of friends; Lucille Moyers and Edna Boulware. Lucille was in the Ariel community and Edna was the organist I replaced at the Monroe City Christian Church several years ago. Guess this was the year that Uncle Albert Bixler died also. He was married to dad's sister, Angelea.

Judy was deciding where she was going after school in Moberly. She finished school in May of 1983 and wanted to get a job somewhere. I suggested that she put her application in at different places and she did, and someone would offer her a job. Sure enough, she got a call from Boone Retirement Center. She was a little disappointed as she said, "I didn't go to school just to pass meds." My answer to her was that, "You have to start somewhere, and this can be a stepping stone to a big job in the future." She finally decided to take the job and I helped her move into the apartment with Kathy in Columbia.

She didn't work very long until she came home with quite a story to tell. She said, "I don't know what the moon has to do with older people, but I've noticed that every time there is a full moon, everyone wants to go somewhere. They are ready to go out any opening they can find, with a suitcase or something with clothes inside."

I have heard of cases like that also, but never thought much about it as I hadn't worked in a nursing home or around older people like that. She said, "It doesn't matter whether it is an open window, door or anything else; they are ready." My answer was, "You never know what God has planned, but someday we might have the answer."

As Judy worked there she decided that she wanted to become a registered nurse. I said a two-year or four-year and she said four-year. I said, "Okay, if that is what you want." Judy soon got herself all lined out to go to school and work. She did well but had to pay like a junior or senior as she had so many hours based on the hours she had from LPN school. She kept on working and going to school.

I tried very hard to get Kathy to finish her education, but she seemed content with what she had and continued to work in Columbia. At this time, I believe she was working for the Agriculture Dean's office.

My schedule seemed to be the same with the usual tasks to do and occasionally some visitors, which was always nice. I never knew what I might be fixing if they were here for a meal, but I always thought of something. One thing we always made sure was that we had meat and that was thought of every night and you can usually find something to fill in the rest.

We had a fairly bad winter with the usual snow and etc. Ivan sold cattle in February or March after he had fed them all winter. There was always lots of meetings at church, CWF, choir and plenty of work to do as organist. I had four pieces to select besides the four hymns every Sunday. God always seemed to help me figure out something to play. Sometimes I would just select something as things went along with the service that seemed to fit with what the minister was talking about. I was so glad I could do that but sometimes my thoughts got me into trouble, not too bad really. I always seemed to make it through.

We were able to go a few days to Bella Vista, Arkansas I believe and be with the Pfanner's. That was very enjoyable.

Our neighbor's, the Lucke's, decided to move to Monroe City and leave the farm and Ivan helped them to get their things ready for a sale. They had been over on the highway for many years.

Several business people died; G.B. Veatch, our lawyer; Hazel Wilson, wife of one of the Wilson's that ran the Wilson's Funeral Home; Harold Kern, who had an appliance store, and from whom I bought a stove that I liked so well. These were all in the early part of the year.

I was excited when we got an invitation to go to a wedding. This time it was the son of Dorothy and Steve's son, Stephen, and he was getting married in Muskogee, OK. That was nice to get away for a night or two. This was a short visit but at least something different. We got to visit while we were there with the rest of the family including Lloyd and Mildred, which was always great, as well as the rest of Uncle Baxter's family. Some of the cousins I do not get to see very often so I took advantage of it every time I got a chance. It was a very pretty wedding.

Aunt Lillian had been in the hospital for a while and was sent to the nursing home and I wasn't told. The things you go through when taking care of someone can be such a challenge to say the least. Aunt Lillian was especially pleased when her sister Etra, and Minerva and W. R., came that summer. Nice to have surprises like that. During the time they were here we had the Watts-Gibbons reunion at the Cannon Dam area and all were able to attend. That was a joy to have all of them here.

August was the Fall Festival and they always had a contest between the little boys and girls for the 'Prince and Princess' contest. To see those little boys and girls all dressed up so cute and to watch their actions, as well as, to play the music for them to walk across the stage to be judged. I was asked many times to play the music. That was always a lot of fun for me. I would only need the pieces that would be fitting for the occasion and just play. For instance, if the little girl had a blue dress, I would play *Sweet Little Alice Blue Gown*. Just an example of what I did.

Fall was here and the usual things; getting colder and you have to make sure that your stock has enough to eat. If they are out on pasture you have to be sure they have some protection from the winter storms. We had many different kinds of stock. Cattle, hogs, chickens, ducks and guineas. None required a lot of work, but if you did something for each, that made the schedule rather busy. Of course, we always put up silage. This was corn silage and mainly went in the silo. That usually meant a man or so; usually a neighbor who wanted some silage also. Sometimes there were as many as five or six farmers that wanted silage, and each would help the other.

We went through November and December and then another new year. Sometimes it seemed the years went by so fast. Every year we always enjoyed the New Year's with Marvin and Lois Lehenbauer at each other's homes, as I think I mentioned before. Throughout the year we enjoyed each other's company like for birthdays and many other times. We would help each other take care of each other's kids in case the other one had something to do that it wasn't the place for the kids. This was off and on throughout the year.

This particular year on January 5, 1985 I had a couple contact me and wanted me to play for their wedding. They were such a nice couple, Harry Boerckel and Helen Johnson. They both had been married before but seemed to be in a hurry to get married and asked me to play for their wedding at the church. How great it is to find someone so much in love and ready to make a commitment to each other. I was delighted to play, and the evening was planned. The wedding was at Monroe City Christian Church and on to the Holiday Inn and back for cake and punch.

The next day was the sixth and I couldn't help but think of thirteen years ago when dad was found on the pond dam dead, west of the Watts place. What a shocker to say the least!

We started having company, Dorothy and Steve Seward from Kansas City, that was one of the Baxter Watts clan. They dropped in quite often but always good to see them. A couple of Monroe City people killed in Columbia; the Lanham's. Mrs. Lanham wrote articles for the Monroe City News.

I was still busy with music lessons, basketball games, and seeing out for mother and Aunt Lillian. Old Man Winter was trying to show itself with deep snow and ballgames galore. Aunt Lillian got to go home today, and she was thrilled. Had help lined up for her to have some help. Moved Carolyn Lehenbauer home today from Warrensburg. Think she graduated.

Ozzie Osbourn died today. Hard to believe he was younger than me and used to live northeast of me out on the highway and was such a great guy. I remember the family well and how Ozzie and Lois always tried to do things for you and so it is hard for me to realize that he is dead. It was thought that he died of cancer and I remember seeing him while working in the field and made me wonder if he was as careful with the sprays as you should be.

He was a State Representative and sure was busy. When he wasn't in Jefferson City at the Capitol he was farming, and not enough hours in the day. This is life and you can never figure out everything as to why so many years left but not supposed to be. Ozzie and Lois and the kids, Lori and Doran, were members of the Monroe City Christian Church. I remember playing the organ and Ronnie Mayes sang. He had such a beautiful voice! There was an overflow crowd. A time when you want everything just right and you work hard and pray that everything will go just the way God would want it to. Sometimes when playing I would call upon the Lord to help me to think of more pieces to play when my list was running short, and you know he did just that!

The same night Ozzie died there was a couple by the name of Roy and Betty Cookson found in their night clothes, in a barn near Bethlehem Church. Why did this happen? What is going on in our communities? A murder one place and then another! One thing about it; God knows even if no one else does. This is sure not the Christian way of life. Another death was Helen McClintock who lived off of Rt. A and was the mother of Reva, Lucille and Nelson. She died of natural causes. Nelson died several years ago. Life goes on and you wonder, "What is next"? I never thought I would live in a community where there were so many murders. That's supposed to be in other communities, not in this one.

Other happenings was a first cousin, Charles Watts' son, was killed in a car accident. This would have been a grandson of Uncle Lonely.

A fun time when we went to a car-show in Springfield, MO. Never saw the like of old cars and of all colors. Lloyd always wanted to share what he enjoyed with me and my family. He was truly a 'Big Brother' to me. Mary Sue's older son

Bruce and 3 girls visited us also and they were such fun. He has a beautiful family! I wondered at the time if I would see them again and if they would remember me. Time will tell.

Kathy came home in May of 1986 and decided to go to Hannibal LaGrange College and worked part time at Hardee's.

As usual, things were very busy with lots of visitors, lots to do, music lessons, gave lots of perms and attended the rodeo in Fort Madison with friends. Anything like this was quite a pleasure trip as a few laughs and change of scenery made a lot of difference to help you to accept so much going on, and yet a way to escape things for a few days just to get away. I'll have to say that the Baxter Watts family sure did break the ice; to help us change our schedule. They were always very supportive of me in all that I did and helped to make my days cheery as well as many of our friends.

I'm now in the year 1986. Aunt Etra, W. R. were here as well as Dorothy and Steve, and the Watts-Gibbons reunion was on a Saturday, June 7th and I was asked to play for a wedding the next day. This was for Lori Osbourn, the daughter of the Osbourn family that grew up next door, and Eddie Easterling who were to be married at the Parkview farm house on the south side of Monroe City. They had a piano out on the front porch and I was to play there. Everything else was to take place in the yard. The wedding was to start at 2:00 p.m. At 1:45 I started the music and I played through all of the music and didn't see a sole and it was nearing the two o'clock mark when I saw someone and asked them to check on Lori and see if she was ready for it to start. This person came back and said, "It will be awhile. She still needs to wash her hair and paint her fingernails." I about flipped my wig and I didn't know what else to do but to just start the music over and I did. After going through it again, and slowly, everyone was ready by that time and I was glad. Many times, you stick in an extra piece or two, but I needed way more if this continued. Everything went well, and they were married, and the ceremony was over. My part finished after a while and it was a very joyous occasion.

I was taking care of Aunt Lillian and sometimes I wondered if some of the family was just checking me out. No comments were made however. I'll have to say that doing for Aunt Lillian and mother was quite a task and sometimes I felt it was running me to death. There was no one else to do it and quite a bit of business to take care of with Aunt Lillian as she was getting some help from the Veteran's and the rest was hers to pay.

Little by little I was getting ready for Lillian's sale and didn't want her to know so sometimes it was difficult. I had dealt with someone staying with her and now she was in the nursing home and it was time to sell her things in the house and sell the house. This was very hard to say the least. Things were just sitting there, and she was paying utilities. I really hated to sell her things and sell the place. I was sort of scared that someone would tell her about what was taking place but luckily, they didn't.

For the sale we had to move the things into a barn in Monroe City where things were auctioned off. Many sales were held there, and I was told it was completely safe. However, I couldn't help but be sort of scared and knew I had to risk something to make a change and relieve her of the bills every month. That sort of went against the grain but it was a must. I also had a person that was interested in buying the house and so after the sale it sold rather quickly, and I was hoping I didn't get any static from anyone. I was told that things should have brought more than they did at the sale, but I did the best I could and that was that. Aunt Lillian did ask about things and I would tell her that everything was fine and that seemed to satisfy her.

Lloyd and Mildred were at the sale, and then went back on Sunday to Colorado Springs. I really didn't expect them, but they showed for a short time. Everything went well, and I was glad when it was over.

In a few days we made reservations at the Landing and camped with our friends, the Pfanner's. That helped so much to just get away.

I had a buyer, which was the Geist's from next door. They were glad and so was I when the final papers were drawn up. I met with Ron and Shelly at the bank and signed the papers for them to have full possession. The bank gave me a check that I deposited to Lillian's account. Lillian every once in a awhile would ask about things and I would answer that everything was fine. I never did lie to her but answered her truthfully. I was so happy I didn't have to keep checking on the house.

I spent quite a bit of time keeping track of her bills; figuring everything to the penny. I even went to Hannibal to get some of her medication to save her money. Throughout all of the above I still was organist, gave music lessons and took part in church, choir and CWF. No one had to rock me to sleep at bedtime.

Time passed quickly, and the carnival was in town and on Saturday night they always had a Prince and Princess contest for ages probably three to six. I was asked to play, and it was fun to watch all of those little boys and girls all dressed up and parading across the stage in their pretty dresses and the guys in their suits. It was a pleasure to play for them.

FROM ONE THING TO ANOTHER

I haven't said much about Marvin and Lois Lehenbauer, who were our neighbors and relatives. We would keep each other's kids, have birthday parties and always spend New Year's Eve together playing cards and all sorts of games. Each furnishing goodies for the party that was first at one house and then the other, for our new year 1987.

The months rolled by fast and before we knew it, it was cold with quite a lot of snow and roads were drifted. Schools were canceled, and decisions had to be made from day to day depending on the conditions of everything. Mother was still in her home and Aunt Lillian in Monroe City Manor. I worked very hard to keep them both happy. Sometimes I sort of felt I was meeting myself coming and going as the old saying goes. I was still holding all of the jobs that I held before and many times I am sure if it hadn't been for God I would have had to give up on a few things.

Easter services were in the latter part of the week and I noticed that Aunt Lillian was not acting right. I had been watching her pretty close and she just wasn't breathing right. I had the nurse to check her and they just said, "Stay with her and watch her. She could go." I began to get rather nervous. Here she was needing someone with her and I was supposed to play the organ for church services at seven. I didn't want to leave her and felt caught in a spot. I had no one to call on; so, I was wanting her to get better, and instead she died just ahead of the services at church. She died at 6:30 p.m. and I had just enough time to get there before the services starting at seven.

People were notified, and services were held at the Christian Church a few days later. A nice crowd at the services.

Judy was in Columbia going to school to be a four-year nurse at the University of Missouri and working too. Kathy was working at the Agriculture Dean's office.

May of this year Ivan had arm and hand surgery in St Louis, and we were told to go to St. Louis University. We had never been in this part of St Louis. The hospital looked okay but everything else was very strange looking. I was told to go across the street and get a room for the night. Frankly, I really don't remember why, but when I got inside the building I was afraid. The railroad tracks were near, which sent chills up and down my spine. The floors creaked as you walked. You heard doors opening and shutting during the night as well as all sorts of weird sounds. I will never forget that night. I turned on my prayers and prayed I would still be alive the next morning. It got dark early that evening and I have never, ever spent such a night as I did that night and hope I never do again. It was awful. While Ivan's surgery turned out okay and he was dismissed the next day, what I went through was enough for a life time.

Julia Lehenbauer, Bennie's widow, died at this time after spending several years in the nursing home in Monroe City, MO.

One of my students that I had taught died, and the person that married us died also. Almost made you wonder about life. For sure, you never know what is going to happen next. Life is full of surprises. This is supposed to be a story of my life and I keep telling about all of those that have passed on. I often think about life and the happenings beyond our control. We must keep our prayers going to the lord and try to live a good life.

Kathy had a little cosmetic surgery on her lip that she thought she needed; so, she had surgery by a recommended doctor that was in St Louis. This all went well, and she was very happy.

The rest of the year was the usual things; among a lot of company after Lillian's death and into the fall.

The Bixler's in California wrote back and forth with us and during the spring we got word from them that they were coming and wanted to see what it was like to live on a farm in the spring. The word came the first part of May and I didn't have much time to get ready for them. I had told Ivan before that they were as close to being brothers as anyone could be, as Ivan's mother was a twin to Bill Bixler's father. I didn't really care, but couldn't help but wonder how in the world I was going to keep things going in the house, cook for all of us and do the work outside and etc? They soon drove in and told me to relax that they would help me to do everything including the cooking.

Bill didn't know the first thing about the tractor and Ivan told me to ride with him and show him how to drive the tractor, as well as disk the field. We started in that small field just east of the barn. After a few rounds Bill noticed that he had lost his billfold. My thoughts were, 'How on earth are we going to find that billfold and get any work done?' Well, I noticed something on the ground about the second round, and there it was on the disked ground and oh how happy we both were to find that; as so many things are hard to replace when you lose them. That made our day very enjoyable to say the least.

Time passed so quickly, and I wasn't ready for them to leave when they did. I think they thought there was sure a lot of work on the farm. We had such a great time together and many laughs.

Mid-June we either got a call from Mildred and Harry Graham or they came up and asked us if we would go with them on a trip to Denmark, Norway and Sweden. I couldn't believe my ears and I didn't know how to answer. We had had so many things going on that I even wondered if we could go anywhere. Ivan and I finally decided to go and the four of us left June 30th from St. Louis for New York. We flew out of New York at 8:35 at night for Copenhagen Denmark.

I had never been out of the states except to Hawaii and wondered how things would go for us. I wondered about Ivan being a diabetic and etc. Leaving New York and seeing the lights along the coast was so pretty, and it made you wonder about a lot of things. As we neared Denmark we saw many statues, islands and canals. We saw very narrow streets and old buildings. Taxes were 108%. Bicycles were galore especially on the corners of the blocks. Before we had been there awhile we were in shops and everything seemed very expensive.

We found that the yellow crop was rape and mustard. Most houses are on farms, and they are run by cooperatives and industrial part. Everything was made of bricks, cement, rocks and clay; local materials. All stock was in confinement homes made from the same material with tile roof. To get from one place to another like Denmark, Norway and Sweden we had to go by boat and the boats or ferries held the car also. I saw a few horses, cattle and some sheep. We saw two tractors with cabs. They believed in God but worshiped different Gods.

Cows were mainly brown and white and no fences except near homes. Some areas the houses were attached to the barns. Lots of shrubs and always a flagpole.

Traveling to Denmark you didn't find any machinery. Everything was imported. A plain bicycle cost 400 dollars, a speed one cost $1,000. Cars cost at least $20,000. Traveling to Stockholm, hay was in stacks. I would rather live in Sweden than Norway. People in Sweden were more one type people. Some ground was very flat and rolling and other more and more hills. Bergen was noted for salmon.

When climbing mountains, it is sometimes very hard to get past cars going the opposite way. Many times, you have to back up a long way or move to an area where you can get past one another. Sometimes the opposite edge is right straight down. A little scary! There was never a dull moment as you rode along on the bus. All in all, it was a very exciting trip and when we came back, we could not find a taxi to take us to our hotel and we were worn out. We had a scary ride and sent to a hotel on Long Island. Some of us didn't have our luggage. What a night! Finally, back to St. Louis and Marlan came after a call.

After some time of some weddings, graduation, lots of visiting with family and friends we decided to go camping with just the family at the lake area. Only the girls and I were around, and we were alone in the camper when I happened to notice that Ivan's mouth was drawn to one side and I was supposed to play for church. I didn't want to leave him and really didn't have anyone that could take my place on the spur of the moment. What was I to do? All I knew was to just pray and have the girls to watch him and to call me if anything changed. Nothing changed, and they didn't call and sure enough he was the same or maybe a little better when I got back. I did take him to Columbia for tests. In a short time, he was able to come home. I did a lot of praying and felt very fortunate that he didn't have a major stroke but maybe a slight one. You can always see the many workings of God if you look or think about it.

Ivan decided to have a certain doctor as his doctor, and he even wore a monitor and was told his heart was fine. I was really disgusted with the answer, so I asked the doctor to tell me, "Why is it that when we go to Hannibal to Wal-Mart, Ivan can go down one isle and up another and then he can't walk anymore? He has to go sit down for a good while before he can walk any further." The Doctor finally decided to do catherization and when he came into the room after doing that you could tell by the look on his face that there was a problem.

He said, "The left side of his heart was completely closed and four blockages on the right." Just think what it would have been like if I hadn't insisted. He would have had a massive heart attack and died probably.

The New Year's party was held with the Lehenbauer's up the road, with some of our kids there. Then by January 2, 1989; one of our members, Nadine Tyree, who lived near the Monroe City Christian Church, passed away. There was a fairly large family and the funeral was held at Garner's Funeral Home and I played for that one.

Nora Lee Lehenbauer, who was like an aunt, died.

Dorothy Colliver, who was my next-door neighbor and lived north of the Watts Homestead, seemed to be there all of my lifetime growing up. She was always trying to give me something like a marshmallow cookie or sweet roll. A mighty sweet lady. I have to mention these ladies as they were part of my life growing up.

So many other death's it seemed. Mary Sue's daughter-in-law, Janelle, who was Kent's wife, died February 13th. It all seemed endless. There were several other deaths but can't mention them all.

It was May when our daughter Judy had an interview for a job at the University Medical Center. She graduated as an RN on May 6, 1989. Judy became engaged to Jeff Raetz and it was decided that they would get married October 7, 1989. Wilma Adams had a bridal shower for her in her home, which was very nice. Wilma was a former neighbor. Time passed very quickly, and they were married in the Christian Church with a reception in the Monroe City High School cafeteria. We had a large crowd in attendance and everything went well. I think someone asked me, "How are you paying for such a large crowd?" My answer was, "Have you heard of paying with your child's inheritance?" That brought a chuckle.

Several funerals and some weddings were off and on the rest of the year.

On June 10, 1989, my niece, Chris and Pat Lehenbauer's daughter Marla, married Dwayne Jones at the Christian Church.

On June 17, 1989, Carolyn Cousin's got married. This is Marvin and Lois's daughter.

On July 9th Steve Seward died, which was a shocker to me. This is Dorothy Watts' husband, or Uncle Baxter's daughter's husband. I don't see that we made it to this funeral, but so sorry for the loss.

On July 12th Judy took her state board's examination to be a Registered Nurse.

On the 26th of July Ivan began having trouble swallowing and they examined his throat and concluded that his throat needed stretching. We were able to stay at Judy's for a night or so, which made it very nice.

Dennis Lehenbauer, son of Lois and Marvin graduated from N.M.S.U., which was really Kirksville, MO. Think we attended with the family.

Had several funerals in the spring; one in March and another in April. This was something that seemed to go on and on throughout the year. Sometimes were like that also.

On June 22nd the Hannibal LaGrange college Administration building burnt from unknown reasons. I remember when I was attending school there we would have to go down into the basement of the building for the cafeteria and I couldn't help but wonder how the wiring was in that area, so I wonder if that could have been the reason.

I was beginning to need help with mother and would go down there and find things that really shouldn't be and so I started looking for someone. Someone told me of a lady near Taylor, MO. I was very pleased with her in every way and she was very easy to talk to. Her name was Opal and we worked out everything and it was such a relief. She was a good cook and such a nice lady! When Opal needed to be off on weekends I would have Mother out here to stay and that worked very well. I always kept my sister Jean informed on things, so she would understand and used her input, but she didn't seem to have much to say or suggest.

October 7th rolled around rather quickly, and I had been busy making dresses, fitting them to the girls that were to be Judy's attendants and someone of the Raetz family was supposed to cater the reception, so things progressed very well.

I don't have very many notes on things happening. I think I had too many irons in the fire with taking care of Mother and Ivan and keeping up with everything else. I know the wedding was attended by an enormous crowd and that everyone got fed and taken care of at the wedding and at the reception, so everything turned out well. Jeff's aunt did an excellent job with the reception and was so very pleased with everything. Opal brought mother, and everyone seemed very happy and that was good.

NOW THE 90'S AND WHAT A TRIP!

The year started off with the usual get together with the Lehenbauer's. The next night was the Graham's and Kathy. Another year starting off with the usual CWF and music things.

Opal had a death in her family she needed to go to, so I kept checking with Mother by phone and offered to bring her out here. I kept watching her as most anything could happen. I knew she was not well. I often called on Jean to come but she said she lived too far away to come. That left everything to me to take care of, which sometimes made it really hard to do. The weather was not great as we had 28 inches of snow on the ground. Goodness, that is a lot! My notes say you could hardly see out of the windows for the ice frozen on them and it was very windy. Gee!

I did take her to the doctor and they did a CAT scan and blood work. Things continued to not get any better and so Mother entered Blessing Hospital in Quincy, Illinois and a dye test was done to make sure there weren't any blockages. Mother has had problems with the rhythm of her heart for as long as I can remember. Appointments made my schedule very busy, but I was able to manage. I thought my sister would come, but she didn't. They really didn't find anything wrong; just her heart didn't always beat right and that made her not feel well.

Several deaths in community and relations when suddenly I got word that W.R. Norton, a first cousin, died on March 9th. W.R. was a first cousin that lived in Texas. He was also the one that wanted me to look after Aunt Lillian. He set up most of her business and I was to carry out her help, care, business and etc.

Jean's first husband, Brad Hulse, died on the 10th and on the 12th mother got to come home. Then, on April 4th mother had chest pains and was taken by ambulance to Blessing Hospital in Quincy and was back home again on the 7th.

Ivan had several appointments and so it kept me busy running. Mary Sue, Dorothy's sister called me and said that both Dorothy and Gordon, her sister and husband had problems. Dorothy had bladder infection and was dehydrated. Gordon was to have hernia surgery. We were always trying to keep up with the other's problems or health issues.

I noted that on July 6, 1990, Jean did stay with mother one afternoon. She finally found the time.

I was still doing music lessons, organist and having all kinds of company.

On June 2, 1990, Dawn Hulse married Jimmy Runyon off the coast of Florida.

On August 14th of this year I got word that Dorothy Seward was dead and I was so sorry, but I knew she had Multiple Sclerosis and wasn't very well. Ivan and I decided to go to Kansas City for the funeral and after the service and burial, we went to a dinner that they were having for the family. Ivan and I were standing in front of Lloyd and Mildred and I got a tap on the shoulder and turned around and Mildred asked, "What is wrong with Ivan?" I turned around and looked at Ivan and his plate was folded and silverware was dropping on the floor. He gave me a blank look and I helped him to a table. I picked up some lemonade and put a little sugar in it and gave it to him. This didn't make him feel better and I didn't know what to do. I called one of his doctors and was advised to get him to Columbia as soon as possible. This was a Friday and no help unless I went to the emergency room but finally got an appointment with a doctor for the 22nd at 9:00 a.m.

We were told that one side of his neck was completely closed, and the other side was almost completely closed with an ulcer. I wondered what was next! He did have surgery and it went well and he was given a chance to live once more. Wonder what else can be blocked and yet live?

On our anniversary, August 21st, I got a call from Opal saying that Mother was standing at the kitchen table with the walker and fell and broke her hip. She was taken to Quincy hospital and after I took Ivan to see the doctor I had to go to Quincy and be with her. She had surgery on her hip and was brought back to a regular room. Gee! So much at one time! Mother seemed to be like herself when she broke her hip but now she was confused and didn't know where she was or what had happened. Opal and I took turns staying with her and spent so many nights there. It was terrible! Jean never did come around even though I called her and told her.

On September 1st she was moved from the hospital to West View Nursing Home in Center, MO. I was told they had a good therapy program there and they would try to help her.

Mother was there several months, and she would not work with them. I stayed as much as possible, but I didn't seem to help either. Jean came a few times, but she didn't have any luck. After three months, the nursing home said I should put her elsewhere for they couldn't do anything with her. I then moved her to Palmyra to Maple Lawn Nursing home and she seemed to do better there. However, she didn't do much walking. I thought many times at the age Mother was, many times she sort of gave up.

Jean was very unhappy when I moved her and said I was trying to keep her from visiting her. That was not my thoughts at all. I had heard good things about the home and that the therapy was so good there and thought it was worth the effort if she responded. I wasn't familiar with any other nursing home so was just hoping I was making the right choice. Several people told me how good they were. Jean was always after me about something it seemed, nothing pleased her. After a few months my time seemed to be so busy and after a few months I did move mother to Monroe City Manor to make it easier on me and maybe that would suit Jean better, who knows?

I took Lois Lehenbauer to Columbia as she had a problem and needed to see a doctor. Marvin was working, and no one was around to take her. On December 20th she had breast surgery. That seemed to go well. I see by my notes that Ivan had something done outpatient at Boone Hospital. Seems like we were always going for something.

Lloyd and Mildred were in Hawaii and called and asked us to come to see them. Lloyd said that they had a place for us to stay, and a car to drive us wherever we wanted to go. I told Ivan about what Lloyd said, and he didn't want to go. I said, "We will never have a chance like this if we don't take it. A place to stay and someone to drive us around." After a few days thinking about it we decided to make the trip. Lloyd and Mildred's kids were to come there for Christmas and leave about the 28th. After giving it a great deal of thought we decided to go, and we did. We left at 7:00 on American West for Hawaii. It was a very cold morning and we flew until 7:30 p.m., changing plans in New York. We were met with lei's in Hawaii and by Lloyd and Mildred and on to a New Year's party and got home at 2:30 a.m. Missouri time. I was a tired puppy! We had a wonderful time and came back on January 13th into Kansas City at 12:30.

The things we saw; the fruit, coffee and nuts, the ocean, and rides we took to see the island were spectacular. The beautiful scenery, whether on land or the ocean watching the whales. Trying to catch one of them blowing and getting that on camera was almost impossible.

Ivan was told by his doctor, that if he drank a small glass of orange juice and ate a half of a banana, he would get his daily quota of potassium. Well, bananas were a dollar a piece in Hawaii, and they are grown right there, so think about it when you buy some here. They are much cheaper here than there. Hawaii is a very expensive place to live and I wouldn't want to live there.

Some of the places that Lloyd took us was to the Haleakala Crater; Tropical Plantation to a Hula Show; Time Share with Larry Welk; Whale Watch; Royal Lahaina Luau; Old Town; Iad Noodle; Portuguese Doughnuts; a local Beach Kenei; Kula Picnic; Tesched; Winery; Whaler's Museum; Golden Dragon; Glass Bottom Boat; Sugar Museum; Fly to Honolulu. We were there ten days and went one place each day plus the sights we saw going to and from.

Music lessons started Tuesday, January 15, 1991, with Todd. War started that day in Iraq and Saudi Arabia. I went to see Mother and my time was really busy with appointments and etc. There were several deaths but none that involved me except to go to visitation. I was doing some cleaning at Mother's as at that time no one was there so needed to get there every once in a while.

I see that John Ritter was installing Dish at my house and so have had that a long time; 27 years.

Every time we went somewhere, and they had two bathrooms; I would say once in a while, "Why can't we have a second bathroom? That sure would be nice to have." So, in April of 1991, Ivan and Marvin started the bathroom in the basement. I was happy about that.

It was in May of 1991 when I received a call from Lloyd wanting Ivan and I to pick up he and Mildred at the Chicago O'Hara airport and then we would go up into Wisconsin to see Mary Sue and Gordon. I immediately thought how big that airport was and to get in and out of that airport could be awful. Lloyd immediately reassured me that it wouldn't be that bad and just follow the signs. Well, I turned on my prayers and hoped we made it; and if we didn't, I didn't know what we'd do. It turned out that when the time came for us to make the trip, with my heart in my mouth and prayers turned on, I did everything right and it could not have gone any better than it did. I was so very happy I was busting my buttons.

We traveled up into Wisconsin and made it fine there also. Lloyd did some of the driving and that helped a lot. I remember coming back Mildred was starving, and we needed a place to eat that would help her with her gluten diet. So, we ate at the Golden Corral and she was very happy about that and was able to get what she wanted to eat; a variety, and that was great.

Lloyd and Mildred were here again in June for a week and that was nice. Had a lot of things going on; weddings, CWF, music lessons and etc.

Ivan had lower back surgery August 28th of this year. Stitches out in a week.

My friend Wilma Adams died today and hard for me to believe. Neighbor, friend and she died of an aneurysm on the brain. I never dreamed she had this. She never told me of her headaches. We made so many trips to ball games at home and in Columbia. We spent so many times together sewing and working on things. That was a hard for me to take.

I'm not for sure whether this is the right spot or not, but I think it was in the fall that I received a call from Lloyd and Mildred saying they are on the East Coast and why don't you come and stay with us and we will see the sights around Washington D.C.? We had a car and a place to stay and so come and we will see the sights. I couldn't believe my ears and said this is too much. Lloyd insisted that it wasn't and so I talked to Ivan and couldn't believe my ears when he said yes to us going.

I knew just like the Hawaii trip we wouldn't ever make it unless it was something like this and so, we did it. We started getting ready and flew to Washington and they met us, and we had a marvelous time. We visited the Tomb of the Unknown Soldier, Jefferson Memorial and the many other sights to see. It was so nice to be with Lloyd and Mildred again on another wonderful trip and so glad I was able to talk Ivan into going as I was surprised that it worked out for us to go. We had never been east before and thanks to Lloyd and Mildred, for if they hadn't talked us into it we would never ever made the trip.

SO MANY THINGS PLUS MOTHER'S DEATH

Our year finished with lots of appointments. The next year started with Lois and Marvin for lunch on January 1, 1992; with Dennis, Rhonda, Carolyn and Jennifer. A few times Chris and Pat Lehenbauer joined us and none of us cared as we always had plenty of food.

Ivan saw Dr. Harvey and entered Boone Hospital, probably about back or hip. He had had surgery on both. I was doctoring with another doctor and they did several tests. Lois Lehenbauer was having tests also. Looks like we are all ailing.

Mildred Harry Graham's just got back from Hawaii. Olivia McClintic, a cousin of Mother's, died. Sam Calvert, a friend of the family, died and I was asked to play for that funeral.

Ivan had more surgery; a quadruple bypass surgery on March 7, 1992. He seemed to have to keep going to the doctor, but at least it kept him going and that was the important thing. He finally got home the fourteenth.

Leslie Gibbons, Aunt Lera's son died. He was the one that looked so much like my dad. The only difference was that dad had a light complexion and Leslie was dark. Lera was one of the eleven of the Watts family.

Jean's son Jim Hulse, and his wife Pat have their second girl. Family is getting larger it seems.

Almost every day I was at the nursing home and could tell Mother was slipping and she didn't know what she was doing or where she was. I called Jean and told her about Mother and we both spent quite a bit of time at the nursing home. Mother died June 22, 1992 about 3:50 p.m., at the age of 95 years. My sister's birthday was the 25th and of course Jean didn't want the funeral on her birthday but waiting until after that was waiting too long. So, Jean thought we should have visitation the next day and the funeral the 24th. It all seemed to be a hurry-up job, but anything to get along with her.

David Henderson was our lawyer and we met at his office, the four of us, to discuss Mother's affairs. Then we went on to Roosevelt Bank in Hannibal where there were some certificates of deposits. We found out there that we couldn't do anything without death certificates.

Things went on for a few days and Jean and I went to Roosevelt Bank and divided up the certificates. We went to the monument place after lunch. The next day Jean called and told me that everything had to be brought back to the house, and if it wasn't she was forcing a sale. I had given her first choice and one of her girls was crying and so she was ordering me this is the way it had to be. I told her I had given her the first choice and now you tell me this! There was a sample, no pleasing her no matter what I did.

Uncle David's son, Leamon Watts died and Ivan and I went to the funeral. He was another first cousin that lived in Moline, IL. Another person to die of cancer, so many of the Watts family had cancer it seemed.

Jean said soon after mother's death that she didn't want a penny of her money going for a nail or a steeple. I said, "There isn't any way you can own a farm and not have to buy a nail or steeple."

Ivan and I discussed the farm and I said, "There is no way I can own a farm with Jean." We met with Jean and Junior on August 24th and the four of us in the Henderson law office and he was able to get everything fixed up without too much difficulty. It was at this time we became the owners of the Watts place.

We worked pretty hard to paint and fix the place up for renting. I did hire some of the painting to be done to make it easier on the two of us as our plates were full without more added on.

Lois Lehenbauer and Jennifer were coming home from Columbia and had an accident between Paris and Monroe City. I made a trip to the hospital in Hannibal to see Lois, but Dr. Phil Foreman had stitched her lip and he thought she would be fine, and she was. A frightening thing to happen! She was the neighbor up the road and we were very close as friends.

The year ended with a group of former HLG students meeting at Rodella (Davis) and Bob Poser's home in St Charles. They had a group of other past students; Lu and Ora Mae Chez, Doris Land Miller and husband, Lola and Lee

Gillium, Willie and Ruth Foreman, Mildred and Lloyd Watts and myself for a wonderful party starting at three o'clock. A great evening enjoyed by all. I guess Lloyd and Mildred were here as I have down and so somebody was with me and probably them. Some of the group had not seen each other since graduating at Hannibal LaGrange in the mid 40's.

Weather was not good come January of 1993. Rain, sleet and snow; so hard to go anywhere. My calendar was filled with mainly CWF meetings and choir.

We were wanting work done here and at the Watts place, so we hired a man by the name of Hobbs that helped us by putting siding on this house as well as the Watts house. That way we wouldn't have to do so much painting. The steps here were bricked out front. I think there was some work done on the porch at the Watts place.

After a few weeks Ivan was sick again and had to go to Boone Hospital in Columbia for a stay. I also got word that George Christenson died, Minerva's husband and the son-in-law of Aunt Etra.

SURPRISE, YOU'LL NEVER GUESS!
IVAN WITH PROBLEMS, REALLY BAD ONES

April 25th was an ordinary Sunday, at least so I thought when I went to church and set up my music for the service. I remember going by the room where they do the fixing of the communion and they needed wine, so I said I would go after it and did. When I started going down the hall to the kitchen and I saw tablecloths, silverware and etc. When I returned with the wine I said, "Boy they are really putting on the dog for someone!"

The lady said, when I gave her the wine, "Why do you say that?"

"Well, they have tablecloths, silverware and everything decorated and so somebody is doing something."

There was something going on, but I didn't know what. Coming down the steps to go to the organ I saw Earl and Reva Rothfuss on one side of the church and Gene and Juanita Pfanner on the other side. That is strange! One a Lutheran and the other one a Catholic? I started the music as it was time and on went the service in the usual manner. After the usual introduction there was a pause and Ronnie Mayes came forward and then I was asked to come to the front and he presented me with a plaque on behalf of the church for twenty-five years as organist.

The plaque says 1968-1993. A beautiful plaque but I really started before 1968. The reason I say that is that I was playing either when or before Rev. Lierle came because I had my first wedding when he was minister. I really think I started before he started which was 1957 when Simpson left and Lierle started.

Nevertheless, it was very nice to be remembered or shall I say honored; for it does take a wee bit of your time to have pieces and practice them for one service. I remember when Rev. Lierle told me how I must play for a wedding. I shook in my boots and thought 'Oh my, I'm not sure I can do that'. Think I told about this earlier in my story.

They had fixed a big luncheon in my honor downstairs and asked us to go first, and we did. I couldn't believe it! The celebration didn't stop there. I was given a book of thank you letters and cards from former ministers and people of the church, all were so precious to me. Then out came a big hanging banner saying, 'Musicians are note-a-able people'. This was done in red and white with red letters and black notes on white in the corners. Someone had put in lots of time on this piece. I was given a sweatshirt with the same saying in yellow and black on gray. I forgot to say I was given a beautiful corsage, and then out came two wooden tubs. I'm not talking about small ones these were the large ones filled with live flowers. They were beautiful and for years they sat on each side of my steps going up to the deck. What a remembrance! A beautiful day to have experienced.

I always said I was going to pay Ronnie back and then he changed health wise so that made it very difficult.

Kathy decided to go to work at Hannibal Hospital and take a few classes at H.L.G. Weather was bad, and she spent a few nights at the hospital even though we were only eight miles away.

Lois needed help, Ivan was dizzy and with CWF and church music that all kept me busy. After taking Ivan off some medication he did feel better, which was good.

Bixler's gave us a surprise visit; after flying into St. Louis and coming here, which was so very nice.

Kathy did graduate in the spring with a Bachelor of Science degree in Human Services.

Judy and Jeff were expecting, and we were excited as it would be our first grandchild. We got a call the morning of July 8th saying come quick that she was in the hospital. When we got there he had already been born; a bouncing baby boy, weighing 6 lbs. 13 oz. We were so proud, and he was named Conor Jeffery. Everything went well and as time went on we got to enjoy him more and more. We even got to keep him a few times. He had lots of hair and I got to give him his first haircut and that was fun.

As time ran on, Ivan was having more and more problems. I remember one night I was going to have Lois and Marvin Lehenbauer here for pizza, and not too long before dinner I looked at Ivan's feet and he had puss between his toes and I knew that I had to do something, and we would have to forget dinner tonight.

I tried to contact the doctor and that didn't work so I drove Ivan to Columbia that night to the emergency room. They said it was just because he was a diabetic and that it wasn't infected. I tried to explain to the doctor, but he acted like I didn't know what I was talking about, so I had to give up and said, "Please give him an antibiotic." He did do that and sent us home.

The next day I began calling the doctor's office and would never get a return call from anyone. I tried several days and different times a day and nothing. I only wanted to know who to go to but couldn't believe no return call. I didn't know what to do and our friends from Hannibal, Harry and Mildred Graham, offered to take us to St Louis to a miracle doctor and my reply was, "It will take one to get him over this."

I said, "I have to go to Columbia and get his records as we have to have them before going to St Louis and they said they would take us there and then to St Louis. What friends we do have to offer to do all of that! I packed a few clothes and away we went to Columbia and then to St Louis. We had a two o'clock appointment with this Dr. Lerwick and it was in the basement of the Missouri Baptist Hospital and we made it on time.

When the doctor looked at his foot he said," My God man, you have gangrene and I am not sure I can save your foot!"

My answer was, "Please just don't send us home."

Ivan entered the hospital and the doctor did surgery. He was a miracle doctor for he was looking after him like no doctor ever has. He was able to remove the infection, fix his leg so he had good circulation in his leg and foot. A wonderful doctor and so glad that we were told by our friends about him. Ivan recovered from the surgery and did well for some time. The surgery was November 12, 1993 and he was able to come home December 9.

January of 1994, Lois Lehenbauer was having trouble with her heart and so she had to go to Columbia and they did catherization on her and she was much better after that.

Weather was bad, but we did make lots of trips to see Dr. Lerwick on Ivan's legs, as the other one was bothering now. Looked like it was first one and then the other. We had been told that the other leg was not good, but the doctor decided to wait and watch, and I really think he thought it best if the surgeries were not too close together.

Laura Belle Felcamp died, also several other deaths. We celebrated several other people's birthdays such as with the Chris Lehenbauer family and so it seemed we were always having family get togethers, but that is always nice.

Our friends, the Graham's, had decided to move to St Louis to be near their son. I hated to see them move, but they were always helping out whether west of Hannibal or in St Louis. Ivan and I helped them some in packing and moving and was glad to return the favor that they had done for us.

The third week of April several of Aunt Etra's family came for the burial of her ashes at the Norton Cemetery. The minister from Monroe City Christian Church, Rev. Delaney, came and was with the family at the cemetery. That made it very nice to have a minister there.

At the request of Dr. Lerwick, I took Ivan to Columbia to the emergency room on the 14th and he was a patient until the 20th. He was wheezing, but no other things were down. Think I probably stayed at Judy and Jeff's and Conor was walking everywhere.

At the end of May Lloyd and Mildred were here for a Center Class Reunion at Hannibal for those graduating the years of 1944 and 45 and then another luncheon at Center at the Grade School gym. The next weekend was the Watts-Gibbons reunion.

Alfred Parson's death. His mother was a sister to mother's mother.

August 9, 1994, Ivan had surgery on his right leg to help the circulation. This was a four-hour surgery. Mildred Graham and Rev. Delaney were with me during the surgery. Came home the 18th. I spent so many nights with the Graham's. Then on October 1st, which was a Saturday, but the doctor let him come home on Tuesday. Bill and Jean came for another short visit.

Come November 12th Jim, Pat Hulse and Jim Robinson were here deer hunting.

Ivan had several meetings with Dr. Lerwick and finally on November 29th, he had to amputate his leg below the knee at the hospital. Finally made it home on December 21st.

January of '95 was so bad weather wise. So many snow storms. Ivan's cousin, Junior Lehenbauer, came over for a visit February 1ˢᵗ and they discussed many things and one was, 'Wonder who will be next, as there had been so many deaths?' The next morning the phone rang, and I think it was Ronnie's wife saying, "Junior is dead!" I couldn't believe my ears, they just discussed this very thing and then get a message like that.

I asked, "What happened?"

I was told that they were cutting a tank open with a blow torch and a piece blew cutting Junior's leg so badly that they could not stop the blood and so he bled to death. They wanted us to know before we heard it on the news. I was thankful they had told us, but so shocked I hardly knew what to say, or do.

I remember having a crock pot of spaghetti and hamburger and so I grabbed that, and Ivan and I went over there to the house. I later got the crock pot back and they said that normally they didn't care for spaghetti and hamburger, but they ate that and sure enjoyed it. I was so thankful that I had it made and took it.

Ivan in a few days got word about a new prosthesis and so we went to St. Louis for that. He had been having so many sores we hope this one helps.

July of 1995, I found a very small lump in my right breast. I went to my regular doctor and he sent me to a surgeon. The doctor wanted me to have a biopsy and I did, and doctor said it was only two or three centimeters in size; a very small growth, but it needed to come out that it was cancer. I have been watching myself for years and hoping I would never come up with anything, but maybe I had found it soon enough that it wouldn't be a problem.

The doctor told me I had two choices; one was a partial and have six weeks of chemo and radiation and the other was a mastectomy. My answer was that isn't hard to answer, "I'll take the mastectomy." Surgery was set up and everything went well. I had a wonderful doctor!

My first cousin, Juanita (Bixler) Cunningham, had cancer on her nose and had to be removed. I'm mentioning this because if you are a Watts, or related, you better pay attention to your body.

The renter's moved from the Watts place and someone had built a fire at the back of the house and it had an aerosol can and it exploded and went through the large window in the dining room. The can landed on the rug and blackened the rug, but luckily it didn't keep burning; it went out. I was pretty angry when I found that. I also had a hard time getting the key back from one of the renter's and wasn't very happy about that. You sure run into all kinds of people when you rent property. Most of the time I have been really lucky, but I began to wonder this time.

Another New Year was welcomed in with Marvin and Lois. I knew Judy and Jeff were expecting and so couldn't help but wonder when it would arrive.

So many deaths I was asked to play for funerals at funeral home and at our church.

March 4th, we received a call saying come quickly and maybe we would make it before she put in an appearance. We hurried and sure enough we made it. We were early enough that we watched the nursery window and the nurse held up a baby in the window in the palm of her hand with only a ribbon in her hair. She had lots of hair, as did Conor, and they added the ribbon and she was looking everywhere. Quite a sight to see!

This was one spring that Hannibal flooded due to so much rain and they put five gates in to keep the downtown area from getting flooded. Years before the gates the water did lots of damage to the business downtown.

THE NERVE OF SOME PEOPLE!
OUR SALE

One afternoon in the summer, a knock on my door, was a neighbor Doran Osbourn and his lawyer. Seems as though a neighbor that moved from Hannibal and was residing west of the hog barns that Doran had built, traveled to Jefferson City and filed a lawsuit against him because he didn't like the odor from the hogs. Doran was very upset, and I can understand why; as I have resided on this farm all of my married life, but if you don't like the smell, don't move to the farm.

After listening to his story, Ivan and I assured him that we would do everything we could to help him and that we understood the situation. I even went out on the porch to tell Doran that to keep his spirits we would stand with him. They left, and the next morning I was listening to the news and it told of Doran taking his life. I was really upset and couldn't help but think, 'What could I have said that would have helped things so that he would not have done what he did?' He was raised close to us; our farms join one another. I knew his family well. He was only forty-one.

I remember taking food to the family, and to see Doran's wife Joy, and those two children. They had a son and daughter. After a few days, funeral arrangements were made, and I played for the funeral at the Monroe City Christian Church. I had played for his dad's and now the son. This was May 20, 1996. Some things you won't forget, and this is one of them.

Aunt Frances died in Chillicothe, MO today. This is Uncle Lonly's wife and we were able to attend the funeral. This is actually his second marriage.

This was the year we bought a new four-wheeler, a Polaris 300. Ivan wanted something to help him get around over the farm.

The work on the farm kept us busy and by mid-September we got word that Lloyd, Mildred and the Laster's were coming, and they wanted us to go to Branson to some shows. We decided to go there and had a great time. I think we stayed in a condo of some of their friends. That was right nice, but a ways to go see the shows.

The CWF had a big salad luncheon and that turned out well and I made my usual pretzel salads. The members fix their favorite salads and people come and can eat all they want for a certain amount. A good money maker for churches.

November wasn't long getting here, and we had Jim and Pat Hulse and Jim Robinson here for deer hunting. So many times, there were more than just three; for there were times that Jim and Pat's daughters and boyfriends came, and I really did have a house full. I did the cooking and always managed to fix something, and no one went away hungry.

One afternoon in the fall I got a call from Dr. Molden, a doctor that I had doctored with, wanting to know where the football field was in Monroe City. I was so surprised to hear from him, and he had a son playing football and they were playing at Monroe. Boy, never know who you might hear from. That particular year the boys played for Class A Football Championship. I never dreamed that they would play a St. Louis team. Guess I wasn't thinking.

I had so many sessions with my grandkids, Conor and Carly, and that was so much fun. I remember one time when I had just Conor and was driving to Columbia and he started singing nursery rhymes, and my but he could sing. Even nursery rhymes I had never heard of and I was so very proud. Later on, as he grew older, he wouldn't sing at all and I was a little disappointed at that but who knows why? Guess he did.

One time I was going to Columbia to take Conor home and he was in the back seat and I was in the front. After some time, he said, "Grandma are you sure you are going the right way?" I chuckled and said, "Well this time I have to go by Mexico to get a part for the Harvestore silo and he said, "Oh." You never know what a child is thinking, and he was actually playing with something and I supposed he wasn't paying any attention.

Ivan had lots of problems with his prosthesis and wore so many blisters. I seemed to always be doctoring them. He was also on a blood thinner so had to keep having his blood checked.

Life was a merry chase from one thing to another until if I didn't check my calendar I would be in major trouble. I don't ever remember forgetting a service or preparing for one, but my calendar kept me in line and looking ahead. God helped me every day to cope with things.

I had another gal wanting to take music lessons and I made time for her, which was sometimes a challenge.

The end of this year the Kendrick's added a ramp for Ivan and that made it so much easier to get up on the deck. Lots of people use it now and so much easier. I was thrilled that they would do it and Jeff, or Eppy as he's known, said it was his first one to build. They did a great job!

The first day of 1997 it was announced that Dee McClintock, the youngest of all of the Bud McClintock family, died in Hannibal. The Bud McClintock place was on the way to Linwood School. I walked by it every day on the way to school.

As time went on Ivan had more and more problems with his prothesis. The man doing the work could not seem to fit him right and that was bad. So many trips and everything was getting costly. You don't mind the expense if it works or fits, but when it doesn't that is bad. Then I started having problems with my knee. Looks like it is catching. Ha! I had Orthoscopic surgery on my knee and it was done in St Louis. Guess too much running and they are wearing out.

So many deaths it seems. This time it was Jim Floyd. I think his wife died last year or so and now Jim. This was the couple that went with mother over to the pond dam to see about Dad. They were dear friends to them.

The 19th of April marked the surprise birthday party for Lloyd Watts in Sierra Vista, AZ. I got there early and got behind the curtain, so Lloyd wouldn't see me. They had everything decorated and I think Lloyd thought that I would show, but he didn't know when. I could not stay for any length of time, so I came on a Friday and went back on Monday. That was really quick for me. When coming home I had my college friend pick me up and I spent the night at her house. The party was really nice, and Lloyd was surprised. This was for Lloyd's 70th birthday.

Ivan had to enter the hospital in St Louis and he had more problems. This time they were checking his heart. They tried the treadmill test and he couldn't do it and they did the one where they put medication in your veins and had trouble there, so they finally shocked him and started him on a medicine called Cordarone. I was staying right in the room with him all of the time at the hospital and he was not eating and not sleeping. I told them, but they didn't believe me. We finally went home after that session and I tried to work with him and hoped he would rest.

Jeff, Judy, Kathy and me worked with him and we never could get him to rest. We had a hospital bed here and he wouldn't stay in it; he would climb over the side. Time came for appointments with three doctors and we saw them and told them how he was acting, and no one said anything about his medication.

On the way home Judy said, "What would you say Mom, if we just took him off the medication?"

I said, "That is music to my ears!"

So, Judy, Jeff and Kathy tried to help me, and we were worn out. After three weeks I said, "We have to do something, we can't go on like this."

Jeff said, "What are you going to do?"

I said, "The only thing I can do. He has to go to the nursing home. You have to go to work, and I have to call the nursing home."

The next day I took him to Monroe City Manor.

Almost immediately his stump started getting red and I was afraid of infection. I talked to the nurses and aides and they listened but didn't change their method of the socks. I put directions on the wall as to how the socks go on and they paid no attention. I went to the special meeting between the nurses and patients and when I requested that the nurse put the socks on or some certain person I was told, "That will never happen."

You would have thought it was impossible and I said, "It is as important as a dose of medication."

But it fell on deaf ears. I was shocked!

Later on, I hired a person that would sit with him for about two or three hours a night, and that worked, and I was happy about that. I was told by a doctor in Hannibal that it would take Ivan three months to get the medication out of his system.

Ivan was in the nursing home at Monroe City from October until December, and a week or so before Christmas I was able to bring him home. And it was January before Ivan was completely normal and himself. I was thrilled then and thought what a changed man! Maybe the New Year will be better than the last one. Let's hope!

We had Lois and Marvin here and then we were ready to take on the rest of the year. I made a decision to doctor with Dr. Zimmerman and quit St Louis doctors, at least some of them. I had enough for what I had been through.

I started giving music lessons to one pupil and played at a funeral now and then. Now and then I would have Conor and Carly and that always made things interesting and never a dull moment. We did have to keep appointments with the prothesis guy and church work, such as choir and regular music.

Carly had her second birthday. Hard to believe how quickly they grow. Conor is growing also and just as quick, it is amazing.

Ivan announced that he was having a farm sale on Labor Day and I was so shocked that I said, "How can we do that?"

"We can't get ready for one than, we don't have enough time."

Ivan thought we did, and talked with Charles Nordwald, about doing the sale.

There were all kinds of reunions. The one held at Rensselaer, Center graduates, and the Lehenbauer one. The first Sunday in June was usually the Watts-Gibbons one. The Center one could be any time and the Lehenbauer is usually July or August.

Those of you who don't know where Rensselaer is; you will find it on HH, near the Big Creek Presbyterian Church. My husband Ivan rode a horse to Rensselaer to go to high school. That was his only transportation. It was too expensive to drive a car and there were no buses taking school children anywhere.

Looking over my notes, I see that a close friend, Helen McIntosh and her husband were here the last of May. Was so good to see them as we seldom see one another as they live near Moline, Ill. There were so many things going on here with Ivan, I couldn't seem to get away by myself or with Ivan.

On July 17th we got word that we have another grandson named Carson. We dropped everything and traveled to Columbia. Such a thrill to see another grandchild and my, but he did have lots of hair! Quite a nice size boy, but enough hair for two babies.

Our CWF had two salad luncheons a year, as they were good money makers. I always fixed pretzel salads. They seemed to go over well, and fairly easy to make. We would have one in the spring and one in the fall.

I guess Ivan had done lots of thinking on this sale and I remember that we had three hay frames full of stuff. I had the bottom of an enamel tea pot that I wanted the lid to. I went to the barns where the wagons were and looked some, but the heat was so intense I was afraid I would pass out, and sure didn't want that to happen. I finally had to give up the search.

I remember the day of the sale, which was Labor Day, that our church was having the food stand and it kept me busy finding things that they needed or having an area for the fixing and serving of food. I also remember I put the refrigerator and the dishwasher in the sale and I got word that Carolyn and Dan Cashman were coming the next day I believe. Carolyn was the daughter of Dorothy Watts Seward. My thoughts were, "How can I deal with company and no refrigerator?"

This refrigerator was one that you had to fill ice cube trays and I decided it was time to get one that did the work rather than deal with the trays. Everything worked out great. Carolyn and Dan came, but they spent the night with Father Mike in Hannibal. The Quinn's and Seward's were great friends through the years. It is always good to see Carolyn and Dan or any of the rest and I just always enjoy fixing for company and for a moment it throwed my mind in a whirl.

I remember that Margaret Raetz, Jeff's mother, was at the sale. Jeff is my son-in-law, and she spent her time holding Carson at the sale. Everything went well for the sale and we had a nice crowd.

My notes tell me that Ivan spent a few days in Hannibal Regional Hospital with fluid and pneumonia. He seemed to have quite a time staying well.

Esther Lehenbauer Freeze, another first cousin, died in St. Louis and the burial was at West Ely cemetery, December 7, 1998.

The year finished with Christmas, doing Christmas plates, Christmas and caroling all in all, a very busy time.

IVAN'S DEATH
GERMANY TRIP WITH THE LEHENBAUER'S

The New Year started off with Lois and Marvin and snow was really coming down. In two days, we had at least twelve inches. Temperature was very cold also.

Impeachment started on President William (Bill) Clinton because of being dishonest and with a Grand Jury.

One of my favorite teacher's Ellen LaRue died and the funeral was at Rensselaer, at Big Creek Presbyterian Church. I was asked to play for the service and I was happy to be able to do that.

I noticed some problems with Ivan's leg and called Dr. Orinoes. He didn't answer and finally after several calls I was able to reach him. I was told to bring him down to St. Louis and he would see him. This was probably the first week of February. Dr. Orinoes was the one that had done the other surgeries and so I thought he would be the right one to call on and after I did that, I was very sorry.

Nevertheless, he finally came to the hospital to see him and thought he needed surgery and took the leg off below the knee. I told the doctor that whatever you do, "Please be sure that you remove all of the leg that is necessary. Ivan could not stand to go through more than one surgery."

Surgery was done, and I was staying right in the room with Ivan and in a week after surgery the doctor came in to remove the dressings and the end of the stump was black in the center. I was so angry, I could hardly stand it. Immediately I said, "When is the next surgery?"

I think I caught the doctor by surprise and he didn't answer for a while, but finally said, "I was so sure I took enough off but guess I didn't."

Ivan had to go for the other surgery and this time it was as if he never did come to. He lingered on and on but began to have fluid and all sorts of problems and it was simply awful. I tried to contact the heart doctor and other doctors but to no avail. I was worn to a frazzle and no one that could help came around.

St. Louis was one place that Kathy didn't like to drive, and Judy and Jeff had their hands full with three children, so I roughed it by myself for some time.

Finally, March 7th, Ivan died. This was on a Sunday about 10:30. I had called the girls and the minister, and he offered to come down, but I felt it would interfere with the morning services so made it through with only the family. Chris Lehenbauer and Gene Howes came, and Chris drove Kathy's car and Gene drove mine. I had thought I could easily drive myself but as we rode along my head would go down. I was falling asleep so was very thankful that someone was driving me back.

The body was taken to Garner Funeral Home and services were set for March 10th, at the church at 10:30. We had an enormous crowd at visitation and funeral. I remember the night of the visitation I finally had to sit down, as my legs would not stand any longer. The Christian Church was putting in an elevator and so requested that Ivan ride the elevator even though it didn't have any sides on it and was so glad that he could.

Money that was given in memory of him I gave to the church; plus, more as a donation for something we needed badly and so happy that I did. Burial was in St. Jude's cemetery, Monroe City, MO.

Carly was only four, when during the service, she got up from where she was sitting and went down to the end of the bench and placed her hands on each side of her face, where she bent over and stayed for a minute or so. She raised up and never said a word. I felt she would be sobbing and I couldn't help but wonder what we could do to help her. When she raised up, she was dry eyed, and sat down where she was before and never uttered a sound.

Margaret Raetz sat in the back of the church during the service and held Carson and you never heard any noise out of him.

Mike and Stephen Seward came the day following the service. I always teased Stephen that he knew if he came here that I would feed him, and he popped in every once in a while. The next day following the funeral was the burial of

Gordon Batley's ashes, which was the husband of Mary Sue Watts, Uncle Baxter's daughter. Burial was in cemetery between Pittsfield and Milton, Ill.

A classmate and husband, Doris and Gabe Sahd and Jack and Elsie Jones were by in a day or so for me to go eat with them. That was nice.

Had a neighbor, Lelah Ogle, to die that was across the road, and was asked to play for the service in Monroe.

The three grandkid's birthdays; Conor 6, Carly 4, and Carson 1, doesn't seem possible. Time waits for no one.

I was asked, probably by the last of March, would I be interested in going on the Lehenbauer's trip to Germany and a few other countries. I was shocked and said, "Yes, I would love to go, but maybe I had better give that some thought as I might say yes too quickly."

I also asked, "How come you are asking me now, when the money was supposed to be in by February or March?"

They said it was because they were short one person. I suggested they give me two weeks, but in a week or less I said, "I will go."

My thoughts were, "When will I ever have a trip like this, with people that I know?"

At least I knew most all of the people that were going and if they were Lehenbauer's that wouldn't be too bad.

My schedule looked way too busy, but I decided to go anyway. In June I even went to Colorado Springs to see Lloyd and Mildred and was gone less than a week but was nice to get away. There were weddings, funerals, music lessons and lots of church work, also family reunions.

I see that money had to be sent in for the Lehenbauer trip by June also. You name it, I think it went on ahead of me leaving on August 5. I had gotten a call from John offering me a ride to St Louis. John's brother Kent drove us so that made it nice to have a ride.

After we got to St. Louis, we all met at the airport. We were flying Continental and were delayed because of traffic.

There were twenty-six of us, and from different parts of the United States, however mostly from Missouri. Our trip was to go to Germany, Austria and Switzerland. Two girls, Carolyn and Marilyn Lehenbauer from Quincy, IL, went the day before to meet a friend; a pen pal in Germany who they had been corresponding with for years and had never seen one another.

Lowell Lehenbauer Williams met us in Newark, NJ, our first stop. Our tour director, Alan Hargreaves, joined us. We arrived in Frankfort at 1:30 p.m. our time; 9:30 a.m. German time. The currency rate was .55579. For example, a purchase of $32.80 was equal to $18.23 in our money. Then on to the bus that took us everywhere on our trip, and the first stop was Rudesheim. The sights were beautiful, but the sun was hot. Saw many castles along the Rhine and many fields which were mainly grapes on the hills along the river. Very few had weeds. We also drove up a winding road to the top of a hill and everything was beautiful to look down on. Everything was neat with lots of flowers in flower boxes on the houses.

Coming back, we were taken to our hotel, The Rheila Hotel Sarne. It was hot, and no air conditioning and no cold water or ice cubes, so we had to be content with what we had. I thought it would be a long 14 days if it is all like this. Two nights were spent in this hotel. Breakfast was ham, cheese and other meats; hard rolls and rye bread. Cereal of cornflakes, oatmeal (uncooked) and puffed wheat. Baked eggs, jelly, butter, cream cheese and chocolate sauce were also for breakfast; you could eat all that you wanted.

The second day, August 7th we made an excursion to Braubach to visit the Marksburg; the best-preserved medieval castle to Germany. After returning we were to eat wherever we wanted, and I chose for lunch a bratwurst sandwich. The afternoon was spent exploring the Drosselgasse, with its quaint wine bars and shops.

For dinner first course was onion soup, roast beef, potato logs, mixed vegetables and chocolate custard over cherries and topped with whipped cream. Lowell and I had a cream puff fixed with fruit and whipped topping but was not good as it tasted like it was sugarless. I ordered tap water and she brought me a green bottle and when I poured it in the glass it was horrible. I read the ingredients and there were several things in it, including magnesium; TERRIBLE! Finally, I found a bottle of water and from then on, I carried it with me and filled it every morning before take-off. I could have cared less if it was cold.

For dinner; beef soup, then chicken with cream gravy and potato croquette and dessert; fruit with whipped topping. After dinner we spent our evening walking around seeing the sights. They had wine tasting and told stories between the different wines. Seven different kinds were given, and the owner played the accordion and sang different melodies, and some were familiar, and we would join in.

We also visited Heidelberg and saw St. Peter's church, The Neckar River and many ruins of the old castles and look-outs. Saw the University of Germany. They were saying that 17,000 Americans live there now. We saw Martin Luther statue and also spot where he held up for his rights. Spent the afternoon touring the city. This was where our picture was taken of the group at the oldest and most notable castle.

We also visited Worms and its cathedral. Ate dinner at the Seppi restaurant. Had red sour kraut (not bad), mashed potatoes and beef with gravy. Had to buy drinks; no water, no bread and no ice and an ice cream bar covered with chocolate and a dab of whipped cream on top.

On Monday, August 9th, a cloudy day. Supposed to be hot, but nice. Taking a back road to the city of Rothenburg. Quaint villages with mountainous landscapes, castles, and forts up high on hills or mountains. Windows in houses tilting at top or open in the middle and folded back. A lot of the houses were stucco, three floors and pointed roof with red slate shingles. Streets and highways were very narrow.

Ottingen Bay means we're in Bavaria. We were met by Mr. And Mrs. Jacob Roettger who showed us a church and graveyard with live flowers on the graves and a stone wall around both church and cemetery. They later showed us the house that was the Lehenbauer home on Milstreet 22, where the original home stood. Barns were right in town, so there was quite an aroma. It began to rain so we gathered in a school room to listen to Frau Roettger talk.

She read a letter from Emil Lehenbauer that was written in 1980. The Lehenbauer's moved because of poverty. Lehenbauer is an Austrian name because it ends in 'er'. We did a tour of the city, and the Catholic Church; the unique St. Jacob Evangelical-Lutheran Church where the Lehenbauer's attended.

August 11th was a cloudy day and it was to be the eclipse at 12:30. We had a four-hour drive to Oberammergau, which is still in Bavaria, also where the world-renowned Passion Play will be seen in 2000. We began seeing green meadows with lots of cows. We stopped at a church which had barn implements, horses and chickens very close, as well as two houses.

We had lunch while the eclipse was going on and ate in a large cafeteria. The guide suggested wieners and potato soup and I had thought I would take both and when the order came there were three wieners, so I took a roll and paid $9 something in deutschemarks. The tour guide, Alan, tried to order one or two, but got three also. We both had a laugh and ate our lunch. As far as the eclipse, it only got rather dark outside and soon it was over.

After lunch we could walk, take a bus up to the castle part-way or a horse drawn carriage. I got a workout on those steps after the bus trip. Quite a sight to see and one I'll never forget.

On the 12th we were to see another castle, very picturesque, and surrounded by mountains with tall pines. This was not far from the Austria border. This is where they had the world Olympics in 1974-76. As we drove along the road, we would see small buildings where they stored their machinery, and if the machinery would have been large it sure wouldn't fit.

On the 13th we traveled to Salzburg, Austria. As some of our group visited with a lady milking the cow, a man was mowing the grass with a motorized hand machine. The hotel was very pretty where we stayed, and Lowell and I went to our room which had a separate room for the stool and the other part of the bath. Lowell had decided to soak her foot and found a pan and drew some water and spilled the water and then fell on the floor.

She said, "I have broken my arm."

I went to her, and sure enough, it looked like she had.

This was ten o'clock at night and she needed to go to the hospital to have her arm taken care of. There were four people that went with her in a taxi cab. I wanted to go also, but instead stayed there and waited until they came back. They were gone for several hours and finally came back, and she had quite a story to tell.

They drove and drove to the hospital and then walked and walked, until finally they found someone that was in the building. Lowell told me that she and I could have done a better job than the doctor did. He even dropped the gauze on the floor and looked around thinking no one was looking and put it back in the drawer.

I was still up when she got back and helped her undress and get to bed. We were plenty tired, but we made it. We visited more cathedrals for music, the statue of Mozart and other composers. Four boys making music on German instruments; bass violin, two mandolins and one accordion on the street.

It was Sunday when we visited the town of Munich. This is one of the safest places to be; featuring the elegant Maximilian Strasse, the Karlsplatz, and the Theatiner Church. The Nymbh Palace had buildings in a circle. There was a fountain of Swans with a large waterfall and flowers. Meals were good.

Next, we visited a concentration camp. Some did a little shopping and Lowell had to have another cast put on her arm. They really put another one over the other one as afraid to take the first one off.

Then on to Switzerland where we rode a cogwheel train which took us 7,000 feet up into the alps to the mountain rail station. This was breathtaking. We had dinner honoring both Lowell's and my birthday, and we each had a card and cupcake and some candy. This was our farewell party and we actually had bread on the table and ice in our glasses. All in all, it was a wonderful trip.

We had gotten to bed at around 2:00 a.m. and were up again at 4:00 a.m. to catch the van at 5:00 a.m. to go back to the airport. We had to catch a bus to go to our plane and were given free tickets for food, but everything was closed. No time for eating anyway! Kent was waiting, and I arrived home around 11:00 a.m. Very nice, but oh so tired! A trip I'll never forget.

After the wonderful trip we were invited to Mitch and GiGi's wedding at Macomb, IL on August 28th. The wedding was beautiful and very pretty and very nice. Not much more to mention that happened the rest of the year, except the usual things with the different seasons; a few weddings and funerals.

GETTING BACK TO NORMAL IN 2000 AND KATHY'S SURGERY

A busy fall catching up after a wonderful trip to Germany, Austria and Switzerland and then got asked to go to Hawaii with Mildred Graham and I just said yes! Maybe shouldn't have but did. Both of us had lost our mates, and we both needed companionship. I figured I should go while I could.

A few days before I left for St. Louis, I was visited by Steve and Barb Seward. They left on Sunday night and I left on Monday for St. Louis. We were to leave on Wednesday for Maui and Marlan was to take us. I was to come back on the 22nd. We had a very relaxing time in Maui. We ate our meals out and relaxed in the sun. We did some swimming in the pool and lived the life of Riley.

After I got home, I decided to make a few changes in my house. Ivan didn't like change and didn't want anything torn up, so I had to forget changing anything. The living room carpet had been down for years and I decided to change that, as well as the carpet in the den and kitchen.

Then it was May 26th when Lowell and Tom Williams came for a short visit. That was so nice to have them. She is the one that was my roommate on our Germany trip. We got to visit others around here that were on our trip also while they were here.

Then in June, Lloyd and Mildred were here and we went to a Studebaker meet in Wisconsin from June 18th through the 24th. He wanted to see his sister Mary Sue and she was in a nursing home in Dorchester, WI. Think this was the trip that Mildred was hungry, and she needed food without bread as she has a gluten problem. We finally got to Hannibal and stopped at "Golden Corral" and she got to satisfy her hunger.

I guess you could say I took off for a visit to Arizona in October. I really felt I had been running around too much but decided to go and get away before winter.

November was the time for the deer season and I have several that come regularly and spend a few days; sometimes getting deer.

All through the year I spent lots of time with the grandkids, and if they weren't here, then I was there and the good times we had together were many.

This might have been the time that I was going back to Columbia with the three grandkids. Everyone seemed okay for some time and then Carly started crying. No one knew why she was crying, and I stopped the car three times trying to make her happy, but she seemed to just cry and each time I tried something else to make her happy. The last time I just didn't know any more to do and finally said, as she was really crying again, I said, "You will just have to cry. I don't know any more to do for you." And she did, on and on and on.

Now the year 2001. Clinton is president, a stamp is worth 34 cents and we seem to have changes in a lot of things. I still keep quite busy as I play cards, dominoes, and work on church music, as well as CWF and many other things.

This is the time that we were working on the basement at church; the kitchen and etc. We had a big project going and spent many hours deciding on things like carpet, paint and how to make some changes in things.

Also found out that Jack Raetz, Jeff's dad, was in the hospital in Texas. They did some surgery on Jack and he kept getting worse and died February 24, 2001. I happened to go by the Raetz home and Carly was sitting on the living room floor playing with her dolls. I was just inside the front door when, she looked up and saw me and said, "Well, God takes them when he wants them, and now I don't have any Pa Pa's and I don't want to talk about it, cause I will cry." She was almost four and that was quite a statement coming from a little girl!

On May 14th I made a trip to Arizona and came back May 24th. I don't remember any particular thing I went for, maybe just to get away and Mildred was always begging me to come.

We also enjoyed the Watts/Gibbons reunion, which is always the first Sunday in June.

All sorts of things going on with the grandchildren, and every so often I was in Columbia keeping the kids. Both Judy and Jeff were working and was hard to do both. Carly was taking dancing lessons and had a recital at 2:00 and a baseball game at 11:30 and both Margaret and I attended. We tried going to most things the kids were in. They are not little but once, and then it is all over as far as the little things. Conor was playing ball also and we attended a lot of his games.

In August Margaret and I took the kids to St Louis to Six Flag's and the Zoo. We had such a great time there.

The next few months several cousins died; Pauline Gibbons, the widow of Leslie and Juanita Cunningham's husband died also in Columbia. So many deaths every year it seemed.

I remember being in the restaurant with a group of friends in Monroe City and they said that the World Trade Center had been bombed in New York City. What a tragedy! To think we have people in other parts of the country and they want to change our lives and destroy whatever they can.

My first cousin's son, Jim Greathouse, died and a neighbor's son was killed. Then in December, Connie, Jack's daughter, died from a heart attack. We seemed to just keep going to funerals that go on and on.

Jack was one of those cousins that we did more things together as we grew older. He often took me to dinner in evenings as both our mates were deceased, and we didn't like going by ourselves. One time he drove several of us to Heartland, near Bethel, MO. A long way from here, but what a buffet they had with all kinds of food. His mother was Ella was a sister to my dad.

Some of our winters were great and others were very snowy and lots of it; closing schools and making it difficult to get around. You usually find it that way in Missouri. Lots of time freezing rain also. I used to never stay in, or at least not much, but now when I see that stuff I stay in because I sure don't want any problem with falling and breaking something.

We got word that Mary Sue, the one that we went to Wisconsin to visit, had died and she was Lloyd's older sister. I think I made it to the funeral in Illinois, near Pittsfield for that. Have no notes as to what Lloyd did.

Prior to Kathy having surgery, she was working at one of the schools and she had trouble walking at times and then sometimes she didn't. Before surgery it took twenty minutes for Kathy to go from the school to her van. Then later, she was crawling to the bathroom as it was too hard for her to walk.

Kathy, my daughter, had back surgery in Columbia on April 9, 2002. I really didn't know whether Kathy was helped or what. The doctor said very little, and that day Rev. Goughnour came for the surgery. It was a very long surgery and I was very worried. I had begged the girls to let me take Kathy to St. Louis and they both said No! Judy told me of how the doctor was a renowned surgeon and I said I hope he is, but I didn't have the faith in him that I would have if it had been in St. Louis. He acted so strange when I went with her to the doctor, and it took forever for him to answer a question.

I stayed my nights with Judy and Jeff and spent my days at the hospital. After sixteen days she finally went to a private room. She could not move her legs at all. The doctor was gone and so you could only ask the nurse if you had a question. Sometimes you got a good answer and sometimes you didn't. I couldn't believe that he was overseas telling others how to do the surgery and then have a case like this that couldn't even move her legs.

She finally got to go home from the hospital on June 17th. She went to Judy's and she and I took care of her for several weeks. In the meantime, I was wondering where we would go next with her. We finally made arrangements to take her to Rusk, a center to help people in Columbia for therapy. I took her to therapy several weeks and then she moved in and they taught her to scoot on a board to get places, such as to get to another chair, to get to bed, to use the bathroom; otherwise she was using a wheel chair to get around. She was given some exercises, but nothing changed and not much helped.

I started calling my doctor in St Louis who was a surgeon and I thought so much of; the one that did my breast surgery. He recommended a doctor that he thought would be good, so I started calling to get an appointment. I know I got an appointment August 8th and was told to be there by eight o'clock in the morning. I was scared, as I didn't know where I was going but we started out early and we were told that morning before we left Rusk that St Louis could not do anymore for her than they could do. Also, we had to get back before nine o'clock and if we didn't the door would be locked, and we could not get in.

I asked, "What about her things?"

They replied, "They will be locked up and we couldn't get in."

With my heart in my mouth we took off and I prayed all the way down there and you know what? We made it! We kept waiting for the nurse to call us in and they seemed to put us off. Every time I would start to go get us something to eat or drink, they would say, "It won't be much longer."

Finally, it got to be 12:30 and we were still not called in and a nurse brought us some chips and dip that was left over from the nurses eating. We ate some because we were certainly hungry. We were finally called in around two o'clock and the doctor, after examining her said he couldn't do anything unless he opened her up and took a look as to how things really were.

He said, "X-rays don't show enough."

The doctor told us to go home and he would give me a call and tell us when we were to come and have a place for her in the Rehabilitation Institute of St. Louis, which is behind Barnes Hospital.

I began getting everything ready as much as I could and when we got the word, which was August 16th, I moved everything out of Rusk in Columbia and headed for St. Louis to the Rehabilitation Institute.

The first night I spent at Holliday Inn and the food was terrible. I knew I had to find someplace else to stay for I can't stand the food not to be good. They mentioned Barnes Lodge and I found that and was pleased with surroundings. I had a safe place for my car and for me and the price was right also. I bought food and took there and put it in the refrigerator and there was a place to cook or microwave if you needed one. I had a regular kitchen to use, and that was good.

I would usually take my car over and park across the street from the Rehabilitation Institute. I was told not to go to my car except in the daylight and I listened to all who talked to me about things. I had different roommates and made lots of friends while there.

They did the Doppler test and found that Kathy had good blood flow in her legs and feet and a good pulse. This made me feel good. She also had the myelogram test and CAT scan. After doing all of the tests they sent her to the Rehabilitation Center and began work on her legs by using the shock treatments.

After this they even had her standing between bars and she gained a lot of strength that way. I found that when she didn't have therapy things were harder for her. They soon had her walking with a walker. It was wonderful to see this happening since I hadn't seen that since before surgery. She continued to improve, and I was so happy, but Kathy had trouble keeping up her exercises when she wasn't there. Kathy was improving as long as she was taking therapy but when I would bring her home she seemed to stop exercising. That was not a good thing. I think she will have problems the rest of her life, but it is so much improved as to what it was at the very first.

I came home every few weeks to catch up on things; still playing the organ but once in a while I called on someone else to take my place. I did play for the funeral of my postman, Leslie Borden. Later Rev. Steve's father died, who lived away from here. There is always someone that passes that is our family or friend.

Come deer season the usual ones were here; the Hulse family and the Robinson family too. I think it was last year that Ashley got a deer. You never know who will and who won't.

2003 started off with snow and doing things for fun. We had a lot of different things going on at church like in the past; CWF, Dominoes, I was still organist and played for the choir, which sort of kept me busy and out of mischief. There seemed to be lots of deaths, reunions, a few weddings and etc.

Seems the worst part of the year was on October 18th, when I was rather excited; as I only had one more window to clean, which was the picture window in the living room, and I would be done with windows for the year. This was the top window in the row, three across and three down. One of the Anderson windows that the storm window comes off and you wash it clean, remove the one below and put the other one back. It's not really hard and my feet were about two or three feet off the ground when suddenly the wind blew really hard and away I went; up into the air and came down with my right leg in a prickly bush.

This was on a Saturday afternoon about 1:30. I knew the front door was locked, neighbors across the road were gone, no cell phone in my pocket and the big trucks were not paying any attention as to someone being on the ground. I laid there for a bit thinking, "What am I going to do?"

I realized I must take my time and not rush into anything and first crawl to the banister at the front steps and then try to pull up and stand. I crawled and that didn't hurt so I attempted to stand, and I could not stand at all on my right leg. This was on a Saturday and I was supposed to play for church on Sunday morning. How could I do that?

I thought of lots of things, but I had to be able to stand and walk on my leg. I tried several times and I could not stand. I had to get to a phone, and finally by scooting backwards I made it around the house and up the steps, across the deck, in the door and to the phone in the kitchen. I called a neighbor and then Donna Mayes, as I sometimes used her husband Ronnie to fill in for me and right now, I'm not sure who I used.

Nevertheless, Donna and Frances Yates came to my rescue as I had curtains in the washer and some other things going. Someone brought the wheel chair up from the basement and I started putting cold compresses on my knee to keep the swelling down and called the girls also. I had to wait until Monday to call my doctor; this was a doctor in St. Louis that I had used before and seemed to be a really good one. I finally got someone in the doctor's office to listen to me and got an appointment on Tuesday.

When I went down to see him, he took several x-rays and said he wouldn't touch me. I said, "Aw, come on doc, you can fix me up, I'm sure you can."

Again, he shook his head and said, "You have to go to Barnes and let a specialist fix it. You have broken the leg in three places and messed up the tibia. I won't dare put you through that, for I might take too long, and you only have so long to fix things."

I was disappointed but knew I must take his advice. He said, "I will call, and you can call also, and we'll get you in as soon as possible."

I finally had surgery at Barnes on October 27th. At Barnes I was in the hospital there for a while and then went to Judy's to rest and wait. I remember that Jeff, Judy's husband, came to my home and got the chair that was Ivan's and brought it to Columbia for me to use while recovering. That was so great for him to do that and I wonder how he was able to do it since it's such a big chair.

I finally got the cast off on November 5th and he put my leg in a brace. The brace came off November 19th because of bruising and swelling and I was to wear only the stocking. Therapy was started November 21st at Broadway Therapy in Columbia. I had a lot of swelling and stiffness in my leg from toes to above the knee. The therapist was great, and we did a lot of work several times a week and I am lucky to be walking to this day.

I went through two weeks with 50 pounds weight and then full weight two weeks with a walker and then nothing. I came home on February 8th, 2004. I drove my car and that felt so funny to be doing that; I was actually scared but made it fine.

One of my classmates all the way through school had died. It was Reva McClintock Rothfuss and visitation was at Garner Funeral Home that very evening. I had to stop and go even though that was very hard in a lot of ways. I remember walking into Garner's and people looking at me as if to say, "Where have you been?" Maybe they didn't know what I had been through. They probably didn't. I felt lucky to even be there.

While I was in the chair in Columbia, I knew I had to have a new yard fence and I made a decision to put in a vinyl fence as I thought it would be less care than some other types and would look great. That required lots of clearing the trees and brush out of the way and finally I was able to get that done and have enjoyed that so much since I had it done. I sold walnut trees and worked hard to clear the way for the fence to be put in. Several people helped in getting the job done, such as my nephew Jim and his friend J.R. They were always coming here for deer hunting.

Kathy became engaged to John Lampton, who she had been dating for some time. Kathy was living in an apartment in Hannibal. It was in January that Kathy, Judy and I decided to go to Quincy and shop for dresses. The girls decided that I should not do a lot of sewing for the wedding, so we bought Kathy's dress and the bridesmaid's dresses too. It was actually fun to see what we could find, and it seemed to be a good time to do this.

Kathy thought she would have the wedding in the fall, but no date had been set. I think I was still walking with a walker and Kathy with her canes. This was probably quite a sight, but we knew what we were doing and didn't worry about that.

Former President Ronald Reagan was buried on June 11, 2004. Later in the fall was the Watts-Gibbons Reunion. Another one of my cousins, Minerva Christenson, died on July 28, 2004. She was Aunt Etra Olsen's daughter. Etra was another one of the Watts family.

Later on, I had the grandkids here to enjoy and took them to the Watts place for them to ride horses. The two older ones enjoyed doing that, but Carson was not too happy about it. This was when the Simpson's lived there.

Kathy and John chose their wedding day to be September 18th and the reception was at the Monroe City Public School Cafeteria in Monroe City, just like I did for Judy and Jeff. I always said I would do one wedding for each of them and if they did more than that it was their problem. We had several visitors; Tom and Lowell Williams from Cleveland, OH, Lloyd and Mildred Watts from Arizona, and Dale and Patsy Watts from Colorado Springs, CO. Some from St. Louis, MO also came, and so all in all, it was quite a crowd.

I was having someone to cater the wedding, and all in all it was quite a group. A lovely meal was done by the Lampton family the night of the rehearsal supper, so all in all it was quite an affair. Kathy had to decide who would give her away as her dad had passed, and she chose Jeff Raetz, her brother-in-law to do the honors. The reception was attended well also, so it was a night to be remembered.

After all of this, was of course, deer season with the hunters and all of the fall things happening.

As we slipped into another year the weather wasn't good in January and February. Lois was having heart problems and later heart surgery. Kathy had a fractured foot from falling. I had a knee that I had surgery on from falling at the front window and had begun to turn in. The therapist and I both kept telling the doctor that the brace should be put back on, but he couldn't see it and it was plain enough that people who were strangers were saying something to me about it.

The doctor finally said he would send me to someone at Barnes who will take care of my knee and I told him, "No!"

He looked at me strangely and I said, "I'm going back to the one that sent me to you."

He replied that he didn't know the doctor when I said his name, and I said, "That's alright. He is good and that is where I am going."

I went back to Dr. Johnson. Surgery was set up for May 25th for a knee replacement. Lloyd and Mildred offered to come and take care of me after surgery and that was wonderful. I really wondered how I was going to manage. They were wonderful to me and I had a therapist and nurse from the county coming through the week also. Lloyd and Mildred were here from June 30th to July 27th. A long time, but they were wonderful and so very caring.

The Watts-Gibbons reunion was held in New London, MO at the Senior Center.

Gene Pfanner, a friend of the family, passed away. Also, one of Kathy's classmates, Brent Perrine, died suddenly. In addition, a first cousin, Lucille Gibbons Brown, died during this year. You never know when it is our time.

My sister, Jean Beedle, was diagnosed with lung cancer. She smoked for years and never thought it would happen to her. She told me first thing that she was going to beat it, but that didn't happen, even after all kinds of treatments. There seems to be lots of deaths.

My first time back on the organ bench was July 17, 2005. Praise the Lord!

Frieda Feldkamp, 98 years old, died September 29, 2005.

I had my first cataract surgery on October 12, 2005 and the second one on

October 25, 2005. I wondered why they didn't do both at the same time, but they didn't, and don't, usually do that.

The rest of the year was the normal things, except shall I say, the candlelight service, which was overwhelming at the Monroe City Christian Church. We had the seats full with families taking part and to see the candles lit all over the seated area, as well as some in the balcony, it was beautiful!

One of my close friends at church, Hortense Henderson, passed away. This was Dwight's wife; the one that I bought fuel from for years and their son was our lawyer for our business. Dwight was the one that asked me to be organist.

We celebrated Carly's birthday and Conor was taking instructions to be a soccer referee. We spent time celebrating birthdays and had a good time together every time we could.

The daughter of one of my close friends from high school called, and informed me that Helen, her mother, had leukemia and her husband had blood clots in his legs. It sounded like neither one of them was in very good shape. I so wish I had gone to see her, as I have wished so many times that I had but didn't.

I felt so many times that I had so many things that were relying on me to do and take care of, that now I wish I had done things different. So, if you are reading this, take it from me, that many things will either wait or someone else will do them. Just go! Don't put it off!

This was the year that a tornado hit Monroe City. Several businesses were bothered and did lots of destruction to the Baptist Church and they had to rebuild the church as there was too much damage to repair.

This was also when Dave and Cindy tore out the kitchen wall between the den and kitchen and opened up the area. It made a huge difference and needed to be done from the beginning.

JEAN, MY SISTER, HAS CANCER

Around this time my sister had more tests and the cancer had spread to her brain and liver. It sounded like it is spreading fast. I soon got word from the daughter of Helen, my close friend from high school, that she died at 2:00 on April 1, 2006. I was so sorry to hear.

Jean, my sister, didn't want to eat and only wanted to sleep all of the time. I visited her many times, but I could tell each time that she was slipping more and more. She didn't seem to appreciate anything I tried to do for her. Jean passed away on June 5, 2006.

Her funeral was June 8, 2006 at the Methodist Church. Burial was not until July 3rd in Vandalia, MO at 7:00.

I made a trip to Arizona on July 6th and came back on the 17th. On July 20th, Jennie Long, the wife of Earl Long, died.

The last of July, Margaret and I attended baseball and soccer games.

Virginia Ann Greathouse-Hulse, Aunt Ella's daughter, a sister to Jack, died and the funeral was at Big Creek Presbyterian church in Rensselaer, MO on August 14, 2006.

The phone rang one Sunday afternoon, on August 20, my birthday, and I was told that Russell Robinson had taken his life. He was one of the deer hunters that came so often and was always great to fix something if it needed to be done. For him to do that is mind-boggling. Kathy and I went to the funeral a few days later. Suicide is such a bad thing when they have so much life ahead, leaving a wife and family. It is so hard to understand.

The Round Robins are a group of girls that all went to Hannibal-LaGrange College. They would write letters and each one that the letter was sent to would add to the letter, until it made the rounds and then start again. A group had been doing this for years, and they added me to their group after they came here in 2006. I asked all of them to come to my house and on September 7, 2006, they did. They were Olive (Whitaker) O'Dell from Texas; Betty (Wyeges) Heidbrier from St. Louis, MO; Becky (Brooks) Waltz from Kansas City, KS; and Polly Wright and Mildred and Lloyd Watts from AZ.

Usually it was just the girls, but Lloyd wanted to come this time, and of course, it was fine. I had my menus planned and things went really well it seemed, and we had so much fun it was unreal. I made my usual tea ring, bacon and juice. Another meal was meatloaf, baked potato, creamed peas, rolls and peach pie. A third menu included a mystery meat with hash brown casserole, asparagus casserole or broccoli casserole. I'm not for sure what it was, but I know we had some sort of a dessert.

They never did guess the meat, which was venison, and they liked it. I was happy about that. They were here from Thursday to Tuesday morning. Sunday, I believe I played the organ at church. Some had never heard me play, so I decided to do it rather than get a replacement organist. I also think that we went to a restaurant in Monroe City for lunch and then came here.

We seemed to be laughing every little bit, and it was fun, and no one was hungry or uncomfortable; or at least they didn't seem to be and never let on. Sunday, we started having visitors and they just kept staying. I thought to myself, "Oh my, I never thought about what we would eat, and have plenty for visitors on Sunday."

I began to think, "Gee, what can I fix without much trouble, and have plenty for everyone?"

I went to the kitchen, and in came Ruthie Foreman and we started cutting up vegetables. We threw something together and asked everyone if they would like some. I think God came through on this one, as I seemed to have plenty and if anyone was still hungry, they didn't say anything, and they acted satisfied. I was delighted to have help in the kitchen and shall I say, "It worked!"

All of this made some really good memories, and everyone was so glad to see the ones that were here. The group from away from here said, "This is the best reunion we have ever had." That made me feel good, and I was so glad I had made the effort to do it. I so enjoyed the group also, as well as the ones that came Sunday afternoon.

The group left here at 6:30 Tuesday morning. I went outside and told them all goodbye and came inside and happened to look by the washer and dryer and there was a very large suitcase sitting there, and they were gone! My first question was, "Whose can it be?"

Lo and behold, the tag showed it was Lloyd and Mildred's. I tried calling three different people, who I thought had their cell phones with them, and no one answered, or they were turned off.

Now what? To mail that to them would cost a fortune. I had to go after them, hoping I would maybe catch them, but really doubted it if that would happen. I got my car keys and started out.

One of the group, I don't remember who, was talking about stopping in Troy. I thought that maybe they might stop there to get gas or something, although I wasn't sure. I never did see them and when I got to Troy, I stopped at the gas station and made a circle through the parking lot and there was no sight of them anywhere. So, I took out for the airport, hoping I would be in time and that I would not be too late.

I made sure I didn't go too fast as I sure didn't want a ticket and that would make me even later. I got to the airport and stopped at their gate and parked in a ten-minute parking place. I ran up to the baggage area where you can check in outside and told them my story and they immediately told me that I had to go inside and tell them. I asked about my car and was told I had to ask the policeman.

"Where can I find a policeman?"

"Right over there," they said.

There stood a very large black woman in a police uniform and I asked her if my car was safe there. She said, "You have five minutes!"

I asked, "What if it takes me longer?"

Her reply was, "You have five minutes!"

I was shaking in my boots, but away I went inside to look for Lloyd and Mildred. I ran up to the desk and said, "I'm looking for a passenger by the name of Watts."

The lady said, "Who?", and I said and spelled the name again.

She acted like she couldn't hear and said, "Who?"

I thought maybe I could see Lloyd as he is so tall, and sure enough I saw him, and they were all standing together and away I went to them. Mildred went with me to the car and she said, "How on earth did you make it here?"

I said, "I prayed all the way and I made it and so that is how I did that." They were so surprised to see me, and I was thrilled to see them. Everyone got home safely that night and that was good and quite a blessing.

When I got home, I found my house unlocked, but everything was fine, and nothing was bothered, so that was great also. I felt I had taken care of a need, and God helped me do it. No one wants to leave their belongings somewhere and have to do without something, even if it's only for a few days, as it causes us problems and no matter how large or small, things matter to us when we don't have them.

Margaret and I visited Carly and Carson's classrooms on Grandparent's Day at Columbia. I don't remember them having that for Conor, but maybe they did, not sure. It is always great to see what is going on at school where your grandchildren are going. All of my times with the grandkids have been special regardless of which one it was.

The rest of the year was spent with friends, classmates, deer hunters and family visiting. All times that meant so much and I don't want to leave anyone out, but if you're reading my story, I don't want it to ramble on and on, as that can be a little boring, I suppose.

In 2007 the year came in with lots of snow, very slick roads and all sorts of things. One of my friends who lived in Hannibal and had done wiring for me and had given me raspberry plants, passed away and I was so sorry about that. It's always hard to lose good people, or shall I say, people who have done things for you and you won't forget.

I finally decided to go to Arizona for a visit and maybe it would get better while I was gone. I left St. Louis on February 8th and came back on the 22nd. That is a long time to stay. I usually went to Columbia and would take a special bus that took me straight to the airport and then wait until my flight was ready. This made it much easier for me and my family. The buses or transits would go to either Kansas City or St. Louis.

One of our friends, Art Buckwalter, who we had played dominoes with and who always seemed to be in a happy spirit, passed away. He will truly be missed.

I went to Carly's baptism on her birthday, March 4, 2007. I must have missed the date of Conor's baptism. I try so hard to remember everything and that is a wee bit of a job.

Carson had soccer games in Quincy and we attended the games there to see him play. The team did really well and that was great to see.

A group met at Fiddlesticks and it happened that the Gregory's were here from Oklahoma. This was enjoyed by all and then we met at my house to make some final plans for the reunion, which was to be on July 1st. That reunion seemed to go well, and attendance was good.

I had a couple come to me and ask me to play for their wedding. They were Mark Lehenbauer, Ronnie and Shelley's son and Amy Meyer, from Bowling Green, MO. They wanted to be married July 7, 2007 at Amy's home where her parents lived. What a beautiful setting! I have never ever seen a home, barn, yard to look as perfect as her parent's place. It was beautiful! Every flower, shrub, and all outbuildings were as perfect as they could be made, and it was quite a sight to see. An organ was put on the porch for me to use and a tent was over the chairs for people to sit and to add some shade. I had practiced on the organ a few days before the wedding. Everything seemed to go well. It was a sight to see!

I did make another trip to Tucson, AZ to visit Lloyd and Mildred from September 10th through the 24th. I came back in time to help celebrate Judy's birthday on September 25th.

Carolyn Lehenbauer died October 13th. She was the one who was on the trip to Germany with the Lehenbauer group. She was a twin to Marilyn and they were both such lovely girls. She died of cancer. We were teasing them on the Lehenbauer trip that they probably didn't eat like the rest of us and so we got to watching them and found they were always eating, and so we all enjoyed a big laugh over that. We decided that their bodies worked different from the rest of us.

I was surprised when I was asked to play for Ronnie and Shelly Lehenbauer's daughter Leslie's wedding. Leslie was to wed Greg Meier of Jackson, MO. The wedding was October 20th at the Palmyra Lutheran Church. I went to see what they had to play on and they had an older pipe organ and a little different from the one at Monroe City Christian, but I thought I would be fine and did practice several times to make sure I had everything under control. The wedding was at 4:30 in the afternoon and the reception was at Quality Inn in Hannibal, MO. A large crowd attended, and everything went well. I was very pleased as I was sort of scared since everything was new to me and I just wanted everything to go well.

OUR TRIP TO ALASKA – WHAT A TRIP!
ALSO, FRIENDS WE LOVE

The church had their Halloween party at the Wilkerson's and that was fun and well attended. The day after we had a storm with tree limbs everywhere, and it was cloudy and windy and cold. All throughout the year I did have cards and dominoes almost every week and so my schedule was busy.

Deer hunters began to show up on November 9th and they were Randy, Rick, J.R. Robinson, Jim Hulse and Derick Suddarth. Later in the month I got to see Carson play Soccer in Columbia. Then I attended the H.LG. Booster Banquet.

The Banquet had Gloria Gaither as the speaker and she was excellent. This was one of the times I met a friend there, Natalie Gibson.

Russell Roellig died. He was a neighbor who lived fairly close and I gave two of his children music lessons. Bertha Feldkamp, whose mother was a Lehenbauer and was a cousin of Ivan's and was married to Eddie Floyd, passed also.

The year ended with the usual things, Thanksgiving and Christmas, a lot of services and bad weather.

The New Year of 2008 started off rather slow and not too much going on. There were dominoes parties, deaths, card parties, choir, and many other things. Pretty quickly it seemed to be Easter, with lots of special services, the breakfasts of the Masonic Lodge, which so many of us attend each year, and our choir sings at the last program on Friday morning. They usually have so many good speakers and those that really hold your attention and know that God is really present for those that really want to listen. We know that God is everywhere, and if we only look, we can find him. He doesn't go with any particular religion.

2008 is the year that I put new windows in the house as I knew that some of the windows didn't fit quite as well as they should, so I wanted to replace them and see if that wouldn't help on the propane I was using for heat. I bought them from a company in Quincy and was very pleased with the job they did, and it did help in the heating of my house.

May 22nd was the funeral for Earl Rothfuss. He was a close friend of Ivan's and was married to Reva, a classmate of mine. Several other funerals around this time, which were Maurice Lucke, a neighbor and Bill Damon, a friend at our church.

On July 25th several of us left for a trip to Alaska. There were, in fact, nine of us; Dick and Lois Disselhorst, Raymond and Janet Taylor, Darryl and Sharon Bode, John Pflantz, Marilyn Lehenbauer and myself. This was such a wonderful trip to take on the Holland American Line. It was a beautiful ship and it was very nice with lots of area to walk around in and the food was delicious, and you could eat anytime you wanted and almost anything you wanted to eat. I only had one problem, and that was I had trouble walking on the boat without touching someone or something. The scenery was beautiful. The mountains, the villages, and everything about the trip. Marilyn and I shared a room and it was nice to have someone to talk to and to do things with.

Alaska was one of such beautiful scenery. It might be mountainous, or it might be a little village; you could see most anything if you were in the right spot, for it changed sometimes very often. Ketchikan has a variety of hiking areas. Deer Mountain Trail begins near the city center and is a 3.1mile climb. They have short kayak trips and Misty Fjords National Monument. You can find all sorts of things to do with all kinds of guided tours in the areas I have just mentioned. They have many places you can fish, but most of us on our trip didn't really intend to do that. However, it sounded inviting.

Another place we visited was Haines. Nestled on the shores of America's longest fjord, Juneau has the massive Mendenhall Glacier and immense Icefields, where they do lots of whale watching. Sitka and the onion domes of St. Michael's Cathedral. Seward (Anchorage), situated on Cook Inlet and surrounded by the Chugach Mountains. This is also where we watched for the bald eagles. We saw a few animals on our trip but not as many as I had expected.

For the most part we all stayed together, but occasionally someone would take off and go on a special trip to see something. Each special trip cost extra to go and see. Special time and special rates. I think that all in all, we were very pleased we got to see what we did in Alaska. Alaska is a very expensive place to visit and

I remember that a gallon of milk cost six dollars. I would hate to have to buy all of my groceries there.

I believe that on my 80th birthday they had a surprise get-together at Fiddlestick's, in Hannibal. There was quite a group there and it was a surprise and at the end of our meal out came a big cake and that was all very nice. There were twenty-six people in all that were there. That was mighty nice to be remembered on that special day.

Andy Lehenbauer was getting married to Jessica Hannant. Andy is the youngest son of Ron and Shelly Lehenbauer. I attended the shower for them, which was at the Palmyra Nutrition Center. I enjoyed so much being with the Lehenbauer family. They don't seem to leave me out of anything and it is a happy time to be with them.

On September 7th the organ at Monroe City Christian Church quit during the service and I had to finish on the piano.

On September 8th, I got in the shuttle in Columbia and rode too Kansas City and met Pat Whitley and we traveled together to Tucson, AZ to Lloyd and Mildred Watts. They picked us up and took us to Sierra Vista, AZ. We always have a nice time and came back on September 22nd.

Kent and Bruce Batley came and visited me on October 6, 2008. We had such a good time together and I think it was the first time they had both been here. That was a nice surprise.

Then on October 14, a group of us had a surprise birthday celebration for Rev. Steve Goughnour and that was at Fiddlestick's. Soon after this Andy and Jessica met with me as they were wanting to get married and wanted me to play for their wedding which was held at Palmyra Lutheran Church. I was delighted to do that for them and they decided what they wanted in the way of music.

We found out that Marvin Lehenbauer died at Mexico on October 19th. His funeral was at Smith Funeral Home in Hannibal on October 22nd.

Andy and Jessica decided to get married on November 8th at the Palmyra Lutheran Church where Leslie was married, and their reception was at the Quality Inn in Hannibal. They had a very nice crowd and I got along just fine. That was thrilling to me, as this particular kind of organ didn't always sound the same to me as it does others and I was more or less scared, but it turned out okay. Amen!

The deer hunters were here and one evening I was able to go to the Hannibal LaGrange Booster Banquet and meet with Natalie Gibson of Vandalia, MO.

After the organ quit while the church service was going on, it was found that the wiring was bad since it was originally wired back in 1927, a year before I was born. No wonder it was bad! A group of the property committee decided that we needed to have the organ worked on and since the Baptist Church had just had theirs worked on, they thought it should be done at our church. I started begging, "Please don't do anything to this organ. It just needs the wire coming to the organ replaced." I begged and begged, but nothing other than having the whole organ worked on would suffice.

They said yes to a man from St Louis, to let the organ be shipped to St Louis and spend a lot of money on it and put a lot of new stops on it and I was told it would be wonderful! I didn't agree but they paid no attention!

It was going to cost $30,000 for work on the organ, and the wiring was about $500 or a little more. No matter what I said it did no good! I was upset, but that is the way it was. I could have cried buckets but that wouldn't have done any good either. They finally took the organ on January 5, 2009. When the organ was brought back, it was put in a different location and now I can only see the audience, for I'm too short to see over the music. Most of us that play are too short. You can't even see the minister or choir or the deacons that come forward after serving the audience.

I had a dinner for Chris, Pat, Mitch, GiGi and family, Micah, Lorrie and boys. We had a nice visit and they seemed to enjoy what I had fixed.

Juanita Cunningham passed away. She was Aunt Angelia's daughter and lived in Columbia. She had cancer.

Mike Studer died. He was found dead inside his apartment at Monroe City. The Studer family was always so good to me. I'll never forget them. The Studer's did my plumbing and furnace work for years.

The organ was brought back at the last of the month, but it wasn't finished. The guy continued to work on it for several weeks. I went there three times to talk to him about the organ and he was too busy to talk, so I asked one of the committee members to please tell me when he was finishing up as I wanted to talk to him. Well, the guy got done and he informed someone else as to what he did, and I was not called. I decided to resign then after that but hung on for a while and tried it and I was so unhappy. I had to keep trying to miss everything he put on there because it didn't sound right. He fixed the organ for a giant cathedral, like in St Louis, and not for our church. I'm still very unhappy with it and did resign after some time, because I was so unhappy. I felt that if they didn't respect what I thought, why keep up the work. I had been organist since in the late 1950's.

Lloyd died today, April 21, 2009. I was so sorry to hear that, but he wasn't doing well and had trouble talking the last time I was there. He tried so hard to talk, but it was very hard to guess what he was saying. He did know me, and I was so glad to see him. I remember sneaking in back of his wheel chair and said his name and he turned around with a big smile on his face. One thing for sure, he knew my voice, but the poor guy could not say anything that could be understood. It was so pitiful to see him like that. It was so hard on Mildred! Lloyd was in a nursing home and wasn't eating much.

When I came home, I found that another first cousin was very sick and that was Jack Greathouse. My goodness! Am I going to lose them both? This is life and you never know. Lloyd was Baxter's son and Jack was Ella's son. Lloyd died just two days before his 82nd birthday.

Some other things that were happening in the United States on May 27, 2009; General Motors was about to go under and they were taking bankruptcy. This was on Monday and by Thursday, Chrysler was about to go under also.

Stamps for mailing letters were going to 44 cents on May 11th.

On June 9th, Elma Lehenbauer, who was Richard Lehenbauer's wife, died. She was in a nursing home and such a sweet person. Richard was a first cousin of Ivan's and lived in Hannibal.

President Obama did nothing to stop the illegals from coming into this country.

In my notes I have that Ivan and I joined Monroe City Christian Church on November 22, 1961. I have said that I was playing the organ before that, as I had been playing for a while when I played my first wedding with Rev. Lierlie.

I know there has been quite a discussion on when we did join as we were attending much longer before we joined. I also had been playing the organ long before we joined the church. Dwight Henderson was the president of the board and he came down here and I was standing on the back step in 1955 or 1956 when I was asked to play.

Kathy and John's divorce was final November 9, 2009. I suggested to Kathy that she buy a condo in Hannibal, as that would be better than paying rent in an apartment. Kathy did just that and has a lovely condo now.

The last of January I made another trip to Arizona. I think that Mildred was more or less lonely and she was always after me to make the trip and I usually did. I stayed for about two weeks and then I knew I needed to get back home. I found out after I got home that Jack Greathouse was really bad and not expected to live. He died February 20, 2010 and the funeral was February 24, 2010. This was another first cousin, and I enjoyed the times we went out to eat and we enjoyed each other's company.

I don't really remember how Mary Lee Anderson Klein and I got together, maybe it was that I had her phone number and used it and it worked. In any event, we made contact and said we would meet at Cracker Barrel in Columbia. This was such a nice visit and I hadn't seen her since she was at a Center Reunion and she was one that graduated with me in 1945 from Center High School. I have tried to make contacts with her since and I have not been successful.

As I ramble along, telling all of the things that have happened through the years, I hope it makes a little sense; but sometimes I wonder as I jump from one thing to another. It is funerals; friends or family that pass. The grandkids or family members or the trips I take, so it is maybe hard to get or understand what all I have been doing. Time brings many changes and I know one thing for sure, I'm not as young as I used to be.

The very day I got the word that Mildred was coming, I got the news that Mildred Graham had cancer and was starting treatments that very day. I wanted to go see Mildred Graham, but so many things were happening I was caught and felt I had to go get Mildred Watts as she was flying to Kansas City airport on the 8th and she wanted me to pick her up there and I did.

Also, that very day I got word that Steve Seward was coming here and would not get to stay long. I was glad he could be here when Mildred was here, as they seldom get to see one another. Steve would be Mildred's nephew. He stayed from Thursday to Saturday. I took Mildred back on the 22nd.

Mildred Graham never did come out of her round with cancer even though she took treatments. She died in mid-May and the funeral was May 14, 2010. She and Harry were so good to Ivan and me. I'll never forget all of the things they did and then, to take me to Hawaii, what a friend!

Conor, my oldest grandson, had his last lacrosse game and I believe I attended with the family. That was nice, and I had never seen the game lacrosse until Conor played. It is a game that only larger towns play.

I usually don't mention a wedding, but this day was different. Our minister was getting married in the church, on Sunday May 23, 2010; after the regular service. A friend of Rev. Steve's, by the name of John Kuklovich was going to marry them. This would be the first wedding that John had ever done. John's wife's name was Alta and they had been friends with Rev. Steve for years. My orders were; as soon as the postlude was over of the regular service, I was to start the Wedding March for Debbie to start coming down the center aisle. Megan, Debbie's daughter, was to be the bridesmaid, and Rev. Steve came from the side and was joined by Trent Garner, as best man. Following the wedding ceremony everyone went to the basement, where they had the reception, and a nice meal afterward.

May 27th was the day I heard, I think, from Dawn (Watts) Grielbelbauer, Lloyd and Mildred's daughter. She wanted me to know that they would be at my place for lunch. I had no idea how long they would stay or anything. I remember I had just done tea rings and they had put an order in for some rolls, so I did get that done. They didn't stay but a few hours and left and I gave them some tea rings to take with them.

They are the ones that have dogs instead of children and treat them as such. They only let the dogs out of car one at a time, as they were afraid they would get away or something. I remember I didn't quite understand but they did let them out a little bit. They treat their dogs like children and I never did know what happened but really think that the dogs got the tea rings instead of Dawn and Doc, but that is only a guess. They never did say anything, I just don't hear from them at any time. It's hard to understand.

Every few years we would have a Center Class reunion and May 29th was the day for that. I seemed to be pretty busy and if I didn't have a calendar to go by, I might miss something and not stay on schedule. I was playing cards every Tuesday night and choir on Wednesday night, besides doctor's appointments and church things.

My youngest grandson was graduating from eighth grade on June 4, 2010.

Watts-Gibbons reunion is the first Sunday in June, and on Tuesday I was to leave for Ohio and visit Tom and Lowell Williams. Remember that Lowell was my roommate on the Germany trip in 1999. I stayed a week with them and saw the sights in Columbus from June 8th to June 15th.

When I arrived at the airport Lowell wasn't there and I had to wait a bit for her to come but it wasn't long before she arrived. We walked to the car and Lowell drove us to their home. They lived in a large brick home. It was two story with a large room with only flowers. This was Tom's area as he loved to take care of his flowers and had lots of flowers there and outside also. Both were retired doctors and seemed to keep themselves busy. While there we visited their daughter Martha and children, which was out on a farm. It was raining while we were there, so we entertained ourselves by playing the piano. The boy, David, was nine and was learning to play the piano. Megan was fourteen and Allison was seventeen.

Also, while we were there, we saw the movie *Chicago* in the big theater. It was very good. We also did a lot of visiting with their friends. Lowell and I went to the Conservatory and saw many plants, trees and butterflies. We attended church and visited with friends and had a very enjoyable time.

On July 16th Steve and Terri were here and more of Steve's family came the next day; Martha, Jim, Carolyn and Dan, and maybe Mike and his son. I'm not sure whether they made it or not but always good to have them and lots of fun. I think that we all attended the Swinkey Picnic at Indian Creek that is south and west of Monroe City. This is an old church where they have services regularly, a Catholic community where they have life long memories.

Ronnie Lehenbauer's family is one that always remembers me and when they have dedication of babies I am invited and that is really nice to be included. They are all so helpful if I need anything and I am glad to be with them. In fact, I feel honored.

I have not mentioned appointments, but I am usually the one that drives Kathy to St. Louis for her appointments and they have been many. She has had to work hard to even be able to walk and she has accomplished much for her work and many trips. I wondered several years ago if she would ever be able to walk, but she is and hopefully she will for a very long time.

As time goes on, I am losing more and more of my friends and even people that went to school those two years I taught in Center. Guess we all can't live to a ripe old age, it isn't in God's plan.

Around this time, I was having work done on the basement. If you don't take care of one's foundation, the rest of you will go to pot and that is the same whether it is the building or a person's health.

MANY DECISIONS IN LIFE CHANGE AS YOU AGE

I gave so many thoughts as what to do about being organist. I wanted to quit, and I didn't, if that makes any sense. Nothing had changed, and I finally decided to turn in my resignation as organist. I think some were stunned and I had a few that begged me not to stop playing.

Did you ever want to stop and yet you didn't? That was me, but I felt I had had enough and on February 12, 2011, I turned in my resignation, which was a hard thing to do, but considering everything, I felt I must do that. On February 13 it was my last Sunday to play as regular organist. Since than I have played occasionally. I'll never get over my love for music. It will be with me until my dying day. I was 82 when I quit. Jolynn Yates is the organist now.

When I retired, I was presented with a clock from the President of the Board, Richard Gosney. JoLynn gave me a package and I opened it and it was a beautiful silver bracelet. I cherish both of the gifts, as well as the notes in cards that were all precious to me. I still play for the choir.

I made another trip to Arizona to see Mildred Watts, and that is always nice to do. I had a long wait in Kansas City as I missed the MO-X bus and had to wait until eight o'clock before I could leave Kansas City. I found a little bit to eat but the coffee was so strong it could have walked alone.

I started doing a lot of work at the Watts place; replacing windows and working on the foundation. By doing windows and paying for them in January, they were much cheaper. I did this at both houses. The windows were the original windows of a mighty old house except for a very few, but none were double panes. A few were put in the front in the 1950's. Foundation Recovery did the work to lift the southeast corner of the house. We also had to get rid of the cistern there as it was seeping water into the basement. I hated to see that go but sometimes you have to do things you don't want to do. The cistern was our only water source while I was growing up and for years after I left home. When we pumped it out, I thought it would never stop as there was so much water there.

A friend of mine's sister, Herriott Ann King, died, and Lois's brother, Marion Wilson, died also. So many deaths, makes you wonder. Some die so young and some live on and on. Life is like that.

Mark and Amy Lehenbauer are expecting a boy, so I attended the shower. It was very nice.

I had renters move out of the Watts' place. We found boards on the ground and Dave immediately told me that I had termites. I called Reliable to come and I knew Guy East as the East family used to go to the Christian Church. Guy had a plan to get rid of the termites and so I went that way, for what I was doing was causing me too much work and I was not getting rid of the termites. After spending so much on the place, I didn't want the termites to get rid of the house.

A close friend, Lola Gillium, died. She was in college with Mildred Watts and me at Hannibal LaGrange and we went to funeral.

There was word of a bad accident between a car and truck on Route J. A lady from New London driving on Route W didn't stop and hit Dave's truck broad side and Dave was badly injured. His body was crushed from impact and he had a mangled leg. This made me wonder, "What is next?" Remember that Dave Simpson is the guy that works for me when he has time. This accident sure made him take off work for some time and he was a year getting over the accident.

The next week Jean Bixler, a cousin in California that visited so much, died. Also, Cindy Sexton Simpson's father died, so more funerals to attend.

Thelma Wright, from Nashville, TN was visiting at Jones and I was invited over for brunch. Another college friend from Hannibal-LaGrange College, along with a few others and it was marvelous to get together as we hadn't seen each other for a long time. Each person had their own life, and all were very different. Thelma was a singer with the evangelistic group and traveled with Dr. Prince at the college. Several of the others were teachers in different areas, as well as different parts of the states, and some in college as teachers. It truly was quite interesting.

Quite a group of us were still playing dominoes.

I decided to make another trip to Arizona to see Lloyd and Mildred. I flew out February 8th and came back Feb 23rd. Margaret Arnold Swearengen was the mother of Betty Lewis and she would come about every month and visit her mother and we were always doing something. One time she took us to the Mexican Restaurant and we had a good time there. They were some of the people that begged me not to quit being organist, which was something, as I mentioned before, was one of those jobs you want to do, but think you're not respected as to your thoughts on the sound of the organ.

The CWF has two salad luncheons each year and one was set up to be on March 16th. Also, on March 24th, there was a death, which was Nanny Howald, who was the mother of two of my friends. A very quiet, easy going lady.

A 70th anniversary celebration for Penny's parents, Mr. and Mrs. Fishback.

Looks like 2012 was a very dry year. Pastures were getting dry and had to move cattle early. Crops were not as good as it was so very dry.

On August 20, 2012, Jim Hulse, my nephew, took me to St. Louis to have my back checked out. I was told nothing could be done for me and the doctor told Jim that if I ever stopped, I would never get started again. They did all kinds of tests and said they would call me after the tests, including the MRI and let me know what to do. Well, they never called, and finally I called them and was told the doctor wouldn't talk to me and the nurse said nothing could be done for me. I was too old. That was a nice happy thought! The doctor didn't do what he said he would do. He passed it off to his nurse and I didn't think much of that.

August 25th was the date that Neil Armstrong died at 82 years old. He was the first man on the moon. He made history.

Ronnie Lehenbauer began feeding hay rather than move all of the cattle home.

I was having quite a time in September as on the 5th they thought I should have a Peng test for eye movement. Natalie, my friend, went with me and I got so sick and the doctor paid no attention and the third time I got sick vomiting I said, "You are not doing anymore!"

He said, "You are not through with the test."

My reply was, "I don't care. I'm leaving!"

And I left in a wheelchair with a pan on my lap and wash cloths in my hand. Enough! Natalie drove me home and I was glad to get there.

Then, the next week, I tripped over the metal strip that pulls the grass-catcher and down I went. I found I chipped a piece of bone off my big toe and had to wear a boot to get over that. GEE!

I did have to have treatments for inner-ear, but only one trip did the trick. The treatment was done in the basement of the Boone Hospital and that worked great. I haven't had that since. Amen.

My next trip was to see Shawn Holcomb, who lived outside of Bowling Green, and her parents came, and I had a wonderful weekend with Shawn, her family and her mother and dad. We went to St. Charles and watched Shawn and the girls do a thirteen-mile walk. What a walk!

The next week a cousin of mine contacted me and wanted me to go to Palmyra to the celebration of the Palmyra Massacre. 150 years ago, all of this took place. Ivan's grandfather was one of the men that got shot at the Massacre. They set the men on the caskets and shot them, so they would fall into the caskets. Doesn't that sound horrible? I'm sure it was. There was quite a crowd there at the celebration.

Kathy needed to go see about her braces, so I took her, as she doesn't like to drive in St. Louis. I always say it isn't bad if you know where you are going, but if you don't, then it's bad.

Looking at my calendar looks like I get on the organ or piano bench quite often. Not a lot of people play either and so for those that do, they get used for sure.

The year 2013 started off with quite a bit of snow and cold weather. Jim Hulse had surgery on his neck, but this went well, and his arm is no longer numb, which is a good thing. We were still playing cards and Judy and Carly took off to Little Rock, AR to a soccer tournament. Church was canceled, which seldom happens at Monroe City Christian Church, this was March 27th.

I met Pat, Jim and Ronnie Suddarth at the Perry Junction on February 2nd for lunch. That was nice, we don't see each other very often. Ronnie's son came hunting with Jim several times.

Looks like I took off for Arizona on the 4th and came home on the 27th. Mildred will start charging me board if I stay too long. I had a doctor's appointment after I got to Columbia.

Galan Lankford, who was superintendent at Monroe City School for years, died and the visitation and funeral was March 6th. The funeral was at the Monroe City School. I didn't go, but I'm sure that a large crowd did attend.

Looking over the calendar there are so many deaths it is unreal. I see where Margaret Arnold Swearengen was going to stay with her daughter in St. Louis, where she could take care of her better. She had a stroke in her home and had some paralysis. I hated to see her go, but she was in the Monroe City Manor and she had a stroke prior to going there. I thought so much of her and her family.

Several others died; such as Alta Yager, Otis Paris, Russell East and Polly Morthland. The first three were of our church and Margaret Arnold and Polly were both from Monroe City.

We didn't have church again on the 24th. The weather must have been bad to cancel church twice.

I decided to buy new carpet and vinyl for my basement as it was badly needed, and I finally got the basement finished. A man from Hannibal was going to do the finishing of the basement. I still can't believe I now have a special place for my deep freezers and a special bedroom area there also. Before, I had everything in the open and nothing very private.

Several more deaths; Charles Anderson, Lois Vail, and Ann Hoar. Then, within a week, Steve Seward died on June 16th. I was so sorry to hear as he was the one that would come when I least expected it; sometimes bringing his wife and sometimes not. I just wrote about Steve Seward and there were two, father and son. Steve was married to Dorothy Watts, a daughter of Baxter and Alma, and they had a son named Stephen Seward. The latter was one that came to my house.

I had several doctors who were favorites and one was a Dr. Pruitt. He had done my breast surgery. He retired in April after my appointment the first week in April. Obama had made the rule that every doctor had to carry a computer around with him to every patient and type in about the visit and Pruitt didn't want anything to do with that and he said that he and computers didn't get along. How unfortunate, for he was such a good doctor, one that was so genuine in his care.

So many friends were dying at this time it seemed. One was Margaret Arnold Swearengen and the funeral was May 11th. We ate many luncheons together. Others were John Creasman, Gene Howes, Lynn Woods, Melvin Kaden and Betty Benson.

Carolyn and Millie were here September 10th and Carolyn went to see some friends and came back and we went to Kansas City, and then on to Arkansas. We spent several days in Arkansas with Dan and Carolyn and then back home.

We had our usual salad luncheon in the fall, which was well attended. Our CWF has two luncheons a year.

My nephew and his wife, Chris and Pat Lehenbauer celebrated their 50th wedding anniversary with a nice group of family and friends in the basement of the Christian Church on October 27th. This was also the evening of a hay ride at Thorndyke's.

One of the banks in Monroe City closed today. That was the UMB bank and it immediately reopened as the Macon-Atlantic Bank. I'll have to say I'm a little disappointed in this particular bank changing again. That is three times and that is three too many.

One of my neighbors, Richard Hess, who lived just south of me passed away. He was a nephew of the Smith family who have lived there for years. A close friend of mine, Duane Gibson, died suddenly in his truck after he got home. So many, so fast, you really wonder who is next.

SO MANY THINGS HAPPENING IN 2014

Now, for the brand New Year of 2014. Through the years how things have changed. I am still playing cards with the group I was asked to join several years ago. We often play at New Years and when all are here, there are twelve of us.

I see that Leslie Long died. He was the husband of Pat and I have known them for years. The Longs, as well as the O'Donel's.

The man that started my basement here and quit for some reason and didn't come back, wouldn't answer my calls to him and would not return any calls to me. He stopped working here and was gone over six months, and I just didn't hear from him no matter how many calls I made or what hour I made them. I finally had a family move in to the Watts' house and the man's father was a contractor. I started the contractor out on a few jobs at the Watts' place and was very pleased at what he did; like replacing counter tops, new kitchen sink and several other jobs and so I asked him if he was interested in finishing my basement.

He said yes, he would do that. He started, and I was very pleased with his work, and so glad to get it finished after all of that time.

Mildred Watts had decided to sell her home and move to Colorado Springs, to be near her children, as two of them lived there. She had decided on a retirement home where she had her own private quarters and she could take her meals in the dining room, if she moved there. Mildred had lots of kidney problems and had a gluten problem also. I was afraid that she might have a worse problem if she moved, but this is what she wanted to do.

I was out there in Arizona before she sold her house and she was sort of disturbed with the way things were going, but nothing goes as well as you think it could when you are waiting for things to happen. She had a lady that was to take care of the selling of the things in the house and so she thought things were getting taken care of.

By January 24th she had sold her house, and when the buyer walked through, he was interested in a few of the things inside and she sold them to him. She had a lady that was going to sell all of the things that she didn't want in the garage and tables were set up in there and the lady was in charge of that. She really had everything worked out and seemed to be doing well when I left.

The months of January and February the weather was not very good. We had snow and freezing rain and church was called off several Sundays. I was in Arizona and didn't get to come home when I was supposed to, as I got sick and Judy flew out to Arizona and came back with me. I was at Laster's for a night or two until Judy came. We flew back to Kansas City and Judy had left her car at the airport. I was happy to get back home. It's no fun getting sick away from home. I remember we had freezing rain on the windshield driving from Kansas City to Columbia. I finally got to my home on March 21st.

Card games were canceled due to weather. Weather was better in Columbia and they started having soccer practice and games. Carson, Judy's youngest, made first team and was the only freshman playing with the seniors in the soccer games. When weather gets better Margaret and I usually attend some of the games.

Becky Brooks Waltz, a former student of Hannibal LaGrange College friend, passed away. Several of the ones that were at my house visiting that one weekend, and we had so much fun, have died. This is unreal, but I guess it is life.

I see where a lady that was our church secretary died. When they went to her apartment she was sitting in the chair and looked like she had just had a cup of coffee. That is quite a shock. Her name was Dorothy Daman.

One of my classmates, Eva Zott, from Colorado, and her husband came for a visit in Center, MO where we went to school. They had their family reunion on Saturday. I was invited to join them for lunch and did. She sort of tricked me and said it was 'Park Day' and instead it was their family reunion. We had a great time together and it was so nice to be with them for the day.

On May 18th, Marla and Dwayne Jones son Augustus, was graduating from Monroe City High School. We received an invitation to the graduation, so Kathy and I did attend and that was very nice. Afterwards, we were invited to their home and that was nice also. It was a time to be with family and have a very relaxing time.

Next was a reunion of the Center Graduates at the Perry Junction with quite a few there. The following day they had the burial of Duane Gibson. She was one of my best friends, who lived in a neighboring community when I was growing up. She married the same year that we did, and they had three boys and a set a twins. She told me to say it that way as it sounds like less kids.

Dennis was at the airport in Texas and collapsed and several tried to revive him. A doctor and a nurse tried also but nothing helped him to respond. Natalie didn't know of any problem that he had.

Judy and Jeff had a party for Carly as she graduated from high school. That was very nice, and a nice crowd attended, the same as they did for Conor.

The next day was the first Sunday in June and the Watts-Gibbons Reunion. My, but it kept me busy going from one thing to another.

Carly had decided to go to Stillwater, OK to college and she and Judy made a visit there to check on things.

Judy and I decided to go to Colorado Springs for Mildred's 90th birthday party and we did make a trip there. We were not gone very long but it was a nice quick one. After my past experience, Judy didn't want me to make the trip alone. We rented a car in Colorado and drove from the Denver Airport. The party was nice, but Mildred was completely worn out and could not stay until the people were ready to leave. She had to bid them good-bye and leave as her strength was gone and she needed to rest.

Judy and I didn't stay very long after her party, maybe a day or so, and then we left. We thought for sure we would have time to visit our friends the Zott's who lived in Castle Rock, CO. But our time was cut short trying to find our way around road closures. We had to head for the airport and good thing we did as we just about missed our plane. When we got to Kansas City and found our car and started driving home, that was when ice formed on our windshield and it took lots of time for us to make it from Kansas City airport to Columbia.

I could not believe that Dallas Osterhout died. He was married to Marjorie and I went to school with both of them.

Mary Ann Howald died. Remember she is the gal that I met at the hospital when I was in there so long before Judy was born. I had heard that she was getting worse and I was sorry to hear that. It doesn't matter your age as to how long you will live. We get some surprises it seems regardless of how old we are. You never know about the rest of life.

Now it was deer hunting season again and time to do a little cooking, for you never know when they are coming or how many.

Mike Schwada moved the propane tank today as we had to do that before building on a garage and changing the drive. I was so surprised when the job got done so quickly. Mike had finished the basement and I was very pleased with his work. Judy, Dave and I did the painting on the basement. Things were beginning to look so much better and of course it is always better to get things finished rather than half done and quit. Ronnie Lehenbauer let us use one of his tractors to move the tank, which was a thousand-gallon tank, and that is a big thing to handle. The Lehenbauer's also helped us with material to cover the ground before putting down the rock and that helped a lot and they also hauled the gravel for us.

October 7, 2014 was Jeff and Judy's 25th anniversary. Doesn't seem possible that it could be that long but it sure is.

One of the gals of the West Ely Community, by the name of Virginia Pflantz, passed away. She and her son were on the Germany trip and that was very nice.

Mildred Watts, the one that I visited so much, the wife of Lloyd, had called in hospice. So sorry to hear that but that is life it seems. If it isn't one thing it is another. I feel she has not been eating enough and that doesn't help the kidneys and now she needs help to handle herself until the end. I kept in contact with the family and found she was not eating and where she stayed they did nothing to help her. My talking did not help as she was ready to call it quits. Dawn had fixed several things for her to eat and put them in the freezer and she didn't feel like even getting them out of the freezer and warming them in the microwave. Now that is bad and the kids, I'm sure, didn't realize how things were.

Mildred died November 16, 2014. The family decided not to have a memorial service of any kind, which was hard for me to understand. The body was cremated, and the family scattered the ashes on top of Pike's Peak as well as one of the tall mountains in Utah, near where Keith and Nancy live. They did this for both parents.

Deer hunters came here looking for deer and both my nephew, Jim Hulse, and Herb Tyree were here hunting, and each got one, so they were happy about that.

Mike Schwada drew the plans for the double garage and I showed the plans to both of my girls as this was being done so late in my lifetime that I felt they should have the say as to whether I do these plans or not. Both of the girls said they looked great to them, so I gave Mike the okay and he started in. It wasn't long before he had the forms laid for the concrete floor and it seemed in a short time that got poured. This was November 20th and then the framework started as soon as the concrete was set up. It was amazing how quickly they got the different stages done. I fixed a number of cups of hot chocolate for Mike and when Dave was here, I fixed him coffee and that made them both happy. I felt sorry for them at times as their cheeks were cherry red from the cold.

One of our card players brothers, Jack Jones' brother Donnie, passed away. I did go to the funeral at Greening-Egan Funeral Home on December 10th.

The Lehenbauer's finished my driveway and Mike finished the garage and I parked in it for the first time on December 26th. I was so happy with the garage in every way. To get something that I have longed for since 1954 when we built the house. Ivan did not want the garage on the house and now if he could only see what it is like and how nice it is to get into the car without going outside. I think he would be very happy but guess I will never know.

WHAT'S GOING ON NOW?

I found my year starting off taking care of the farm papers, income tax, and many other things. I had noticed last fall that on both sides of the ground near the creek, that hay was sown, and they had bales of hay on both sides of the creek. I had thought I would ask Shuck about this but seemed to not get it done. The ground was not fit for anything more than hay.

Shuck was supposed to tell me about anything unusual going on down there, and he didn't mention anything. I happened to say something to David Simpson about the hay and he said that he had seen Shuck feeding it to his cattle so that is probably what was going on. Dave and Cindy were down there eight years and they had watched things going on down there all of the time they were there and even afterwards.

I played for the Nursing Home in Monroe City, to bring a little entertainment to those listening. I see that Richard Hagan played also. He played the trombone while I played the piano. We would be making lots of music and really jazz up the place. That was fun to do and brought many smiles to the faces of those around us.

March of this year was when I told Ronnie Lehenbauer I wanted him to take over everything. I had been farming 50-50 and it was such a struggle to sell the grain, so Ronnie offered to rent the ground at so much per acre. He offered me so much and that was more than I had been offered before, so I decided right then to go with his offer. I am still with Ronnie and am so happy with the way he does things I don't want to change.

Since this year started, a student of mine from Center, MO passed away. I was invited to and attended a dedication of Andy and Jessica's little girl.

The Lehenbauer's brought cattle here to go on pasture. My time seemed to be real busy trying to keep up with everything.

For some time, I had thought I would have a group of Kathy's friends here that she had been friends with since high school days. So, I set the date, April 25th and invited them. I think there were eight in all, and I planned a very simple meal and worked on it most of the week. Everything went well, and we had a ball! I never laughed so much in all of my life as I did that night. It was a riot! I told them I needed to have them back, so I could laugh some more as it is so good for people to laugh. Most of us don't laugh enough. I won't tell you what time I got to bed. Ha!

Well, I am still playing cards. Most of us are getting up there in years and we often wonder how much longer we will be able to continue. Most of us are in our 80's and 90's.

One of my neighbors, Irene Schachtsiek, passed away. One granddaughter and one grandson took music lessons from me for some time. They were both good students.

Looks like I played at the Nursing Home in Monroe City on Monday, and my classmate's husband died in Colorado.

I had the experience of being out of breath and could not help but wonder, what is wrong with me? I would be so short of breath I would sound like I had just run the hundred-yard dash, but I hadn't. This started probably in January or February of this past year. I talked to the nurses at the doctor's office of my regular doctor and they said, "Call your heart doctor." I would but would be given an appointment for two or three months away. I would not accept that, and the weeks would go by and nothing would change. I didn't have it all of the time but quite often, especially if I would go to Wal-Mart, which was not walking very far from the store as I would try to park a short distance.

I called my regular doctor's office several times and they finally said, "Go to the emergency room." So, after this happened several times, I did ask my daughter Kathy to take me to the emergency room in Columbia. She did, and they told me that the top of my heart was not beating with the bottom and that was why I was getting out of breath. They put me on some medication and I went home with my daughter Judy, who lives in Columbia. I had sent Kathy home as it was supposed to storm, and I didn't want her to have a problem going home.

I think it was June 22nd before my daughter Judy's schedule and the doctor's schedule were together on the date that they would shock my heart and try to get it back in rhythm. One shock and my heart was in rhythm, and I am still in rhythm and so that is great news. I am still on Xarelto to help keep it in rhythm and will probably have to take that the rest of my life. No one told me that but that is my guess. The medication keeps me from having a stroke.

On June 28th I was invited to a Center class reunion by Darrell and Millie Lennox at their home. It sure was good to see the many students of Center School there.

One of my classmates and her daughter, Eva Zott and daughter Linda, met me at Fiddlestick's and we had lunch together. That was nice as she being in Colorado and me here makes it difficult and I won't travel anymore now since I have trouble getting around.

Our minister, Rev. Steve Goughnour's last Sunday at the Monroe City Christian Church was September 27, 2015. I believe that the Nutrition Center catered the lunch we had for Rev. Steve in the basement of our church. We had a regular program fixed out for him that day and it was very nice. He had to retire before the age of 70 from the ministry or lose part of his pension, so he retired. He and Debbie are still in Monroe City, and enjoying retirement while working other places.

Many more deaths of friends here recently. Also, we had the privilege of hearing Donald Carter, who was a timothy of our church. What a minister he turned out to be! He was raised not far from here and his message was indeed a good one. I was so pleased to get to hear him and to meet his wife, as it had been so very long since the last time I saw them.

I received a call from some relatives. One of my first cousins, Linda Beildspacher, her sister Karen, from the state of Washington and Linda's daughter, Cindy Allen from Boise, Idaho. These were Aunt Etra's grandchildren, or Minerva's daughters, and granddaughter. They called and asked if they could come and visit me and also go to the Norton Cemetery where most of the family are buried. I didn't mind and was so happy they called. Linda had been here before, but her sister Karen and daughter Cindy had not. Linda was from Grangeville, ID.

We had an enjoyable time together and everything went fine until the time came when they were going to leave, and they left and went down the road and came back with a flat tire. I called and called, and no one had a tire that would work on their car. They did not even have a spare tire and I could not believe what was happening. Even JC's in Monroe City didn't have one and no one had a solution. This was a rental car and finally I took them to their motel and a man from a place in Quincy, IL came for the car. I felt really bad about the whole thing, but after so many calls that was the only thing we could do.

LAND IN DISPUTE, PEOPLE STEALING AND ALL SORTS OF THINGS

I have been going to the Watts place for years, checking on things, as it seems anymore that some people do not have any respect for those that have land. They think they can trespass on anyone and it is fine. Sometimes they do whatever they want, but I'm afraid I really don't feel that way. I always try to respect others and their possessions. Everyone is dead except me; Dad, Mother, my sister Jean and Ivan. I was given lots of support from my girls and Jeff.

Oh, how I wish we had done more when this first happened in the 1970's. I was not pleased with what the lawyer said and felt from then on this would come back to haunt us and sure enough it did. Mother and I did see a lawyer but were not happy with things. He kept assuring me that this would be okay. The lawyer said, "He can't do that. Tell him to go to Hell."

Mother said, "I can't do that."

The lawyer said, "Yes, you can!"

We will just wait until he starts moving in on the land and then we will go after him. Dad had bought the property across the road on the west side known as the Herron place in 1936. A man by the name of Pennewell was the one that said he had had it surveyed and there was too much land in one field, and he was taking some of it. Mother's taxes stayed the same on the same acreage, and nothing changed.

When I noticed in the year 2013 and 2014 that someone was doing some hay near the creek on both sides, I thought I would ask Shuck, but failed to do so. He had promised that he would tell us if anyone started moving in on the land starting back in the 70's, and we felt we could trust him. After all, he was doing the farming on the land. In looking at the records, the land that Pennewell bought was not sold until 1987 at the court house door, which we knew nothing about that either. I also found two people that saw Shuck hauling the hay to his cows that were on pasture at my farm, on the Watts place. So, I supposed it had to be Shuck that was doing the hay.

In the year of 2015 I noticed that some ground had been plowed and something else was going on and I called Shuck and asked him to meet me down at the Watts place. He said he would, and we met October 25th down there along the road.

Shuck said, "I didn't do that. Hufford did, and he is farming for Bob McClintock."

He had supposedly bought the ground in 1987 and was just now farming it. That doesn't make any sense to own something twenty-eight years and just now farm it. I owned it for the fifty-one years before he bought it, and it took 28 years more before he started farming it? In fact, I had farmed it except the grassy strip since 1936. A total of 79 years! Does that make sense?

Maybe he was trying to slip in and move over a little every year, so I wouldn't notice it. Whatever he was doing it was not right. I even asked him if he would like it if I measured his field, and if he had too many acres, I would just take some and leave him the rest. He didn't answer that question at all. I tried to buy the land from him and his price was unreal.

Since all of this happened; gates, panels and all sorts of things have disappeared. I don't know how anyone can do all of this and have a clear conscious. Nevertheless, all of this happened and even more.

There is one thing for sure, God is always watching, and he knows who did what, and no one needed to tell him. No matter what we do, we don't put anything over on God.

Things finally went to trial and even though I gave lots of material to the lawyer it turned out that Bob won the case over me, which I am sorry to say, but that is the way the cookie crumbles. It took the judge months to give the verdict and I feel things were not presented right for an outcome like that. The judge said she couldn't even tell I ever owned the acres. I had maps that showed dad owning all the way to the creek. I also would not have known any land was in dispute if it hadn't been for Ronnie Lehenbauer. I guess Shuck thought I knew, which is no way to treat the person you are working for. He was very dishonest.

The year ended with bad weather, and some of the people that are supposed to fill the pulpit didn't show. One was a lady from Kirksville that didn't show because of bad weather. Finally, the first Sunday in December Don Carter was our minister for the day and he is one of the timothy's that came from our church. What a minister he turned out to be and it was such a joy to hear him!

The rest of the year was the usual holiday things and church services. Some deaths also, the way of life.

Our New Year started off with a card party, and one of our players had a spell at the party and we were all very worried and she was taken to the hospital. We have often said that so many of us are so old that if something starts happening to some of us, it is hard to say when it will start, as our ages range from the 70's to 96. Two players are 96 years old. Well, so far so good, and will see what will happen next.

Next was the death of one of my friends, Tressie Shively, I was sorry to hear, as it is for so many and some, I haven't said anything about. Nevertheless, Tressie has had several of her family members get married and I was asked to be the organist for them. That seemed to work out just fine and she was always so happy about things. I so enjoy doing for people that are happy about what you try to do.

I remember going to choir and I had a letter to mail and stopped at the post office to mail the letter and had the creepiest feeling go over me and thoughts of get it done and leave quickly. I did just that as I felt there was something that was going to happen, and they were really close. I hurriedly mailed the letter and came back to my car and I drove to the Christian Church for choir.

The next morning, I heard about a shooting in Monroe City and a policeman was shot in the leg. Sure enough, the shooting had taken place just a block from where I was at the post office. On the side street, the man that had shot the policeman was just behind the post office and was holding a gun on a lady and child. I guess it was the voice of God telling me to quickly leave because I was suddenly scared and didn't know the particulars about next door.

My thought was, "Thank you, God!" Have you ever had something like that to happen to you? Don't you feel it is the voice of God?

Laura E. Lehenbauer Townscend died. This was Bill and Nora Lee Lehenbauer's daughter. Also, Sarah Feldkamp celebrated her 80th birthday at LaGrange, MO.

Another first cousin, Wallie (Wallace) of Linn Creek, MO, died. He was the next to the last one of Aunt Lera's family. The funeral was in Hannibal, with burial at Grand View. I found out at the funeral that Aunt Lera had eleven children. Her second girl died at age two or so, at a small age, her name was Marietta. I had not heard of that before. Boy, you can always learn of something new it seems.

I had the pleasure of taking Carly, Carson and Keeley to lunch at Manchester's in Columbia in mid-March of 2016. We had such a good time and it is always nice to be with nice young people. I believe this is when Keeley's mother joined us.

This is the year that I tore up my bedroom and said it was time to change bedspread, curtains, paint, and give things a different look. I don't do this very often, but every few years I usually give something a different look.

May 22nd was the baptism of Emery, Mark and Amy's youngest, at Lutheran Church in Palmyra, with brunch at Old Stone House. That was very nice. I have always tried to attend all of the celebrations that the Lehenbauer family had. They have been so very nice to me in every way and doing things I won't forget.

The Watts-Gibbons reunion was held the first Sunday in June at Essig's. I also got to see one of my former students, Don Krigbaum and his wife Linda, also Ada Krigbaum, who was married to Francis Krigbaum, who was in my class in high school.

July 7th Rex and Pat Gregory, from Enid, OK, came by on Thursday and stayed until Sunday. This is the couple that I met on the Lehenbauer trip to Germany. They have relatives in Illinois and stop here as a break from riding. Always a fun couple to have around.

July 9th was the funeral of Marjorie Osterhout's at Center cemetery and then lunch afterwards at Marjorie's sister-in-law's, Linda Osterhout's. I was able to attend the service and have lunch with the friends and family. Marjorie was in my class in high school. I have visited with she and Dallas (Peck) many times in their home. I was so sure that I would go to Jefferson City and find where Marjorie was staying but never seemed to get it done, which I am sorry about.

Now I wonder, "Why do people put off visiting people?"

My friend, Natalie Gibson, had heart surgery July 12th and seemed to be doing fine. I did a lot of praying, as you never know how things are going to turn out.

She did fine, and I was so happy she did. I was able to visit her when she went to the nursing home before going home.

July 24th Mary and Carolyn, both of Dorothy Watts Seward's girls, were here and that was so very nice, and we had a marvelous time together. I have it down that they were here for dinner. Carolyn wanted to see some friends in Illinois and Mary went with her. I think they spent the night here and then left the next morning for Kansas City and then Arkansas.

I know that the Watts house was not rented, and I believe they were working on the bridge below Brush Creek Hill, when I called a family to see if the road was open. In talking to this family, I told them that I had been making lots of trips to the Watts house, and was getting tired of going around, rather than over the bridge. She said the bridge was open.

Her next question was, "Don't you have renters in the Watts house?"

I replied, "No, it isn't rented yet."

Within a very few minutes I received a call from the neighbor lady's daughter and she asked the same question and my answer was still no, it isn't rented. She asked if they could see the house and I said yes, you sure can. She told me that her daughter and son-in-law were living in the basement, and they are wanting to move. They were soon there, looking at the house, and wanted to move in. We decided on the rent and they were given the keys to move in. Everyone was happy about that, and this way they would be close to her parents. The renters had one little girl at the time.

The Fishbacks, the new renters, were wanting to paint the walls downstairs. I said okay, I really don't care. Just be careful. They worked long and hard to get the work done. I had the walls an off-white color, which goes with most everything.

August found us with another reunion of the Center graduates at the Perry Junction for lunch. That was nice. You never know who you will see or what you will learn.

Sunday, the day after the reunion, I attended a shower for Kayla Hulse, who is Jim and Pat's youngest daughter. That was nice, and she got many lovely things.

Every so often I play the organ at church when the organist wants to be away. I love music and will do it with pleasure, as I enjoy it so much. The position of the organ is the pits and having to miss all of the additional stops does not make me happy, but outside of that, it is okay. I just wish nothing had been done in the first place.

I had a note or so from Sharon Wisner Nelson, saying she and her husband were coming sometime and would maybe stop by. Months passed, and I really thought it will never happen and I got fooled. I received a call from Sharon saying they were in a big truck and were headed for St. Louis and would stop by. This was August 26, 2016. I really wondered, would it really happen. I hadn't seen her since she was in fourth grade, in 1948-49. This would be unreal!

She had sent me pictures of her and her husband and both had snow white hair. I have never turned gray, although my hair is much thinner than it used to be. I received another call about 1:00 or 2:00 saying they were at Chillicothe and hoped they would be here by dinner time. My thought was that they would be early enough that I could take them to Fiddlesticks for dinner. Well, it got to be 5:30 or 6:00 and I was afraid that they would be late enough that I could not take them to the restaurant and so I got out meat, green beans and some potatoes and started cooking.

I think it was 7:00 or after when they arrived, and I felt it was too late, so we made it on what I had cooked. I wasn't exactly proud of what I fixed but it was food and they seemed to enjoy it, so I was happy about that. I had trouble with my potatoes, but the rest was okay.

Jim Hulse, my nephew, Sister Jean's son comes over, or at least contacts me every once in a while. He mentioned that his daughter Kayla was getting married and they were wondering if I would play for Kayla's wedding.

I said, "Sure, I would be glad to do that for her wedding." Then I was asked by Kayla if I would play, and she seemed thrilled when I said, "Yes, I would be glad to do that."

The wedding was to be held at St. John's Methodist Church in Linn, MO at four o'clock. The wedding was beautiful, and the reception was very nice also. I had never been in the church before but was hoping everything would go okay. They had both an organ and a piano in the church. The organ had several things pushed up against it and the minister said, "Oh, just play the piano." So, I have no idea what the organ sounded like and thought it best if I didn't try under the circumstances. Jim, my nephew, said they had rooms all set up for us (Kathy and me) to stay in. That was nice, and they did have the rooms.

After all of the above I got a call around noon saying, "This is Bruce. Would you care if Kerri, Kristy and I come to see you?"

I answered, "No of course not. I'd be delighted."

I think they were partly on their way and thought it would be fun to come here and I was thrilled to see them. The girls had really grown up and Bruce looked good also. We had quite a visit and I invited them to go to a restaurant near here and we would have some lunch. It was about 2:00 and I knew they were very hungry, and I got in with them and away we went. We all seemed to enjoy the meal and most of all the visiting.

Next thing on the docket was our salad luncheon. We usually had two a year; one in the spring and one in the fall. I made my usual pretzel salad and made two. I used to make four but for some reason they think that two is enough and so I did that.

November 11th Jim Hulse and Herb Tyree came for hunting. Herb had wanted to see his niece that used to be in Monroe City near the Christian Church. So, I invited everyone here for a meal including his niece, Susan Tyree, and her boyfriend, plus my daughter Kathy. I learned that evening that Susan Tyree's boyfriend was the son of a student I had in fourth grade in Center, MO. He couldn't believe that I had been his mother's teacher, and I couldn't believe that he was her son. What you learn as you go through life is amazing! I had another simple meal and they all seemed to really enjoy it.

As I wind down in this last year, I can't believe everything I have gone through in all of the years. After the celebration of Rev. Steve Goughnour's retirement we have been going along without a minister all of these months. We have had a hard time selecting a minister, as there are not that many to select from and some do not want to come to a small town like Monroe City. We had a few that did a trial sermon, but some liked it, and some didn't. You know how it goes, no two families judge alike.

We finally chose a minister from Oklahoma, and he was seven hours away. He was a minister for those in prison. He arrived on January 4, 2017. He is not married but has been and has some children. One Sunday his daughter and sister came to visit him, and the church. His name is Rev. Mark Sewell. Rev. Mark did his first Sunday January 8th.

The third Sunday in January was too icy for us to have church. I know due to my condition of back and legs I really hesitate to get out when it is slick as I sure don't want to fall.

I had an appointment with my lawyer, and then in a few days, it was the Inauguration of President Trump, who won over Hilary Clinton for president of the United States.

The trial date on this land dispute was January 26th in New London, MO at the courthouse there. This was something new to me and I had done so much praying and trying to get some material to my lawyer in the last few months. I could not help but wonder how it would go and I felt that it was a little shaky, for anything I gave to the lawyer I felt would probably not be used. I had never, ever been around a trial of anything and it was an entirely new thing for me.

We had to wait on the judge to come, move to another place in the courthouse for the trial, and after a long while we finally got started. I couldn't help but notice how one side had so many more papers than the other side, and the other lawyer was even borrowing papers from my lawyer to turn in, which didn't seem fair.

To make a long story short, we had to wait at least an hour and half for the judge to come back after lunch. I thought that was terrible but said nothing. We finally got started again after lunch at 1:30 or 2:00. It was way after lunch. The marker for my field, near the creek, was removed by McClintock with his old equipment. This is the same type of marker that you find in all corners of land and is supposed to be against the law to remove anything like that. Bob was able to get by doing as he pleased.

I think it was March 17th before we heard the outcome, and that is a long time. My lawyer had failed to show I ever owned the land in the first place, which didn't set well, but that is what the judge said in her writing about the case. I did a slow burn, but it is what it is, and you have to take the judgement or file a claim to redo the trial; and I didn't want to do that. I just wanted it to be over and time will tell what happens in the future.

Ronnie Mayes, of Monroe City, fell and broke his femur at the Mexico Veteran's Home. The poor guy was having quite a time and he died February 9, 2017. The man had the prettiest voice and the many funerals and weddings we did together was mind boggling. They were still asking for him after he had gotten to where it was very difficult for him to follow the music and so I had to turn down several requests that families had asked for us to do.

One of my good friends in college at HLG was Polly Wright. She died February 24, 2017 at age 94. There are not many of us left, but there are a few. God is taking us one by one it seems.

On March 11th I decided to invite the whole Ron Lehenbauer family here for dinner. This was a Saturday night, and everyone came except Shelly, for some reason she stayed home. That was fun, and they all seemed to enjoy the evening. The kids were all so mannerly.

May 21st was Carson's high school graduation. It doesn't seem possible that the last one can be graduating from high school.

May 24th, Lucy, the dog, died and that was sad. She will be greatly missed.

June 3rd of this year I was asked to go with a group of kids that attended grade school in Center while I was teaching. I was to ride with Darrel and Millie Lennox and they were meeting others at the Perry Junction to travel to Herman, MO, where Mrs. Crone lived. I think there were two cars of us that went, besides Lennox, there was Neuschafer, Charlie and Joanne. That was an interesting day and very nice.

I had an interesting question asked of me, and that was I was asked to play at Tom Fitzgerald's 90th birthday celebration, which was June 11, 2017 in the basement of the Christian Church. I said I would, if I could do it, and my playing would be my gift for Tom, as I didn't know what to buy. They said yes, and I did just that. It was a joy to play all kinds of pieces and see the joy in people's faces as I played different tunes.

We had our usual yearly Lehenbauer reunion date the first Sunday in July at West Ely. They said the crowd was small but at least they were able to have it. I missed as I was having trouble getting around with my back and legs but hope to go this year.

Every week we are having cards, but we often wonder how much longer we will be able to do this as we are all getting old and older. Ha!

Had my first shot in the back for pain by a Dr. Meyer, and it did absolutely no good at all. I tried him once more and it worked and got some relief.

I so enjoyed what the children put on for Natalie Gibson's 90th birthday that was held at the farm. They really had a large crowd and it was quite a celebration. This was at the farm where Natalie grew up on the Fred Moyer's farm that is owned by one of her son's.

I had a terrible thing happen and could not believe my ears or eyes. I could hear water running and could not tell where the water was. I went outside on the deck and it wasn't there, so I came inside and went down into the basement and there it was coming out of the wall. This was in the north wall about two feet from the north-east corner of the basement. I couldn't believe my eyes! How could this be?

A stream about two inches in diameter was coming out of the wall and I ran upstairs and called the water department and asked them to turn the water off. They came and did just that and now I had water on the floor of the basement and what a mess! My basement was so nice and now this! I called Ronnie Lehenbauer and he called Jeff Raetz, my son-in-law. I called Judy and she said, "You must have a company to clean up the water. Do not try to pick it up Mother!"

I think she called Serv-Pro. By mid-afternoon in came a green truck and a guy came to the house and he was with Serv-pro. I think there were two people in the truck and he wasn't long starting in the basement cleaning up the mess. They kept carrying motors down the steps and I finally asked how many motors did you put down there and he said 26 fans were placed down there to dry out the carpet. There was water in every room except the bathroom and it was dry, but that floor is a little bit raised so that made the difference.

So many things got wet and it sure took days for them to get it all taken care of and dried and cleansed. I'll have to say that Serv-pro worked diligently to clean up the mess. It did take a while for them to get it all done and their final task was cleaning the carpet and I'll have to say it was a job well done. I never mentioned that I also had someone call a guy from Monroe City to do the digging outside and find the leak and that was done also, and a job well done. I feel very fortunate that I had insurance and I paid the deductible and the rest the insurance paid and that was good.

A neighbor's daughter, Judy Dexter, died. She had cancer and the funeral was October 7th and the Christian Church did the meal.

October 13th, I had another shot in my back and this time I sure hope it works. It did, which was wonderful.

More funerals of friends Joann Burris and Harold Olsen. Seems like it is one after another and where you know so many people it keeps you going to funerals.

I was so happy when Judy and Jeff suggested that I ride along and go to Enid, OK to the Gregory's. They are one of the families that I met on the Lehenbauer trip and they have begged me over and over and I keep saying I will come and this was a very nice surprise. Enid is not far, maybe two hours from Stillwater OK, where Carly goes to school.

I spent two nights with the Gregory's and then the Gregory's drove to Stillwater and we went to Carly's apartment and visited and then on to a restaurant for lunch and then I came home with Judy and Jeff. Emily, Carly's roommate, ate lunch with us also. This is Carly and Emily's fourth year at the college, with a veterinary science major, and both will graduate in May of this year.

One of our card players died at Willow Care Center. This was Alfred Brocaille, Annie's husband. After this death there has been so many things to happen to the players that I am writing this month's later, as there are several player's that are having problems. I am really not for sure when we will start playing again, if ever. One has bone cancer, another cancer of the throat, another pneumonia and now heart problems, and another with a stroke. All we hope is that each one will improve and no one else will have a problem.

After I had been playing for weddings and funerals for some time, I started writing down the names and where the funerals were and the wedding's also. The first wedding I did, I do not remember the name of the ones getting married but do know that Rev. Lierle was the minister. Not counting this wedding, I have down 58 weddings and 180 funerals that were at Ariel Christian Church, Wilson Funeral Home, Garner Funeral Home and Monroe City Christian Church. I'm not mentioning this to brag, just happy that I could help in some way to make someone happy, or to comfort them in some small way.

I want to thank God for such a wonderful life I have had. I am so thankful for my family, friends, my church and all I have been able to accomplish for others. I have felt many times that maybe I made someone happy with music, helping out with weddings and funerals, and other times just playing, like at nursing homes and at gatherings that some enjoyed hearing pieces of all kinds.

To those that read this, may you realize that God has many plans for us and many things that we can do through others and that we must realize that we all need God in our lives. So at least weekly we need to go to church and worship him, Our Savior, Jesus Christ. If not, we can worship by reading the word or watching a service on TV. We can always find a way if we want to.

May God Bless each and every one of You.

Wanda Lehenbauer

ABOUT THE AUTHOR

This is the story of Wanda Watts Lehenbauer, a gal who was born in Northeast Missouri. She grew up on a farm and learned to work hard at a very young age. Wanda was always asking questions and puzzled her parents many times. All through life, Wanda enjoyed doing things for others, loved music and through working on melodies, was able to teach herself to play the piano. Sometimes, when she was bored and didn't know what to do with herself, and whether it was cold or dark or both, she would find the piano and see what melodies she could play. Wanda took a few lessons, and found that with God's help, she could do most anything. Wanda believes that we all need God in our lives and by having Him to call on, it is amazing what you can accomplish.

Made in the USA
Monee, IL
24 May 2020